WHAT PEOPLE ARE SAYING ABOUT VOICES

One of the most vital elements of living a victorious Christian life is the ability to spiritually discern the voices that may be influencing us. Whether it is an external voice urging the listener toward a certain mindset, philosophy or belief, or the internal voices of an individual's mind and spirit, this book will open the eyes of the reader to more accurately determine which messages to embrace and which ones to reject. This is an important book for the days in which we live.—APOSTLE JANE HAMON, PASTOR, VISION CHURCH, SANTA ROSA BEACH, FL

In the climate of our nation, it is essential to differentiate the voices that we hear. In this writing, Apostle Robert Gay successfully equips believers to distinguish the noise of voices. Identification always brings illumination. You will see confusion unmasked and learn how to filter the clamor. Following the right voice will always produce life. The most exciting part is that this teaching doesn't end here; we are guaranteed a sequel.—PASTOR KENNY MECKFESSEL, THE RIDGE OF SHERWOOD, SHERWOOD, AR

As an experienced apostolic/prophetic leader for many decades, Robert Gay has great experience, wisdom, insight, and balance when it comes to the prophetic. Not only that, but he has built a strong apostolic church which gives him a practical biblical perspective. This much-needed book serves to equip, guide, and grant illumination to all who desire a better understanding of prophetic ministry. I highly recommend it!—DR. JOSEPH MATTERA, U. S. COALITION OF APOSTOLIC LEADERS

In a day that there are many voices coming from many directions, we have a responsibility to be aware of the only voices that matter. Dr. Robert Gay teaches us how to steward the voice of God in our lives in such a way that we are not distracted by voices of division and chaos; but instead, we are led by the clear and concise voice of heaven. I encourage everyone to take the time and not only read this book but apply this book to every area of their life.—PASTOR JOSH PICKETT, ABUNDANT LIFE ⟶ ⟶ ⟶ ⟶ N CENTER, MARION, VA

D0880622

Now as much as ever, believers of every stripe need to learn how to discern the voice of God. Inch-deep discipleship, biblical confusion, and sheer prophetic mayhem has left the sheep without a shepherd—we can't seem to tell when God is speaking, and when He's not. In his new book *Voices*, Apostle Robert Gay brings some desperately needed clarity and correction. The recent and widespread disappointment within the Charismatic/Pentecostal church has led to damaged faith and disillusioned seekers. *Voices* is a step toward healing those wounds, and I cannot think of a more trusted leader than Robert Gay to show us the way forward. This book is a gift.—**PASTOR CASEY DOSS**, THE RAMP SCHOOL OF MINISTRY, HAMILTON, AL

If there is one thing I have observed over the last several years, it is we have a real issue with people in the Church listening to incorrect voices. In *Voices* we are given biblical pattern and practical praxis on how to discern and decipher the legitimate voice of the Lord from all the illegitimate voices that attempt to shout at us on a daily basis. This book is a must read and a prophetic call for us in this hour to attune ourselves to hear correctly.—**PASTOR JOSHUA GAY**, HIGH PRAISE ORLANDO, FL

In his book, *Voices: Hearing and Discerning When God Speaks*, Dr. Robert Gay lays out a clear and practical teaching on how to distinguish illegitimate voices from legitimate voices. I, as well as my organization, have benefitted greatly from this revelation. If applied, I am sure it will be a great blessing to you too.—**WILL OWEN**, AUTHOR & PRESIDENT/CEO JETBOATPILOT.COM, PANAMA CITY, FL

After more than a year of fake news, rampant misinformation on social media, and a deluge of false and unfulfilled prophetic utterances, Dr. Robert Gay's latest book, *Voices*, is a welcome and timely word for the Body of Christ. In it, he details how believers are able to rightly discern the voice of the Lord from amongst a cacophony of discordant and deceiving voices, and how to reclaim New Testament prophecy away from the perversions that many of us have witnessed in this season. This book will encourage and challenge you, and my prayer is that it is a vessel that God utilizes to illuminate truth from falsehood and deception.—**JASON REED HARRIS**, CYBERSECURITY ARCHITECT, ORLANDO, FL

HEARING
AND
DISCERNING
WHEN GOD SPEAKS

VOICES

DR. ROBERT GAY

Melbourne, Florida USA

Voices—Hearing and Discerning When God Speaks
by Robert Gay

With a Foreword by Bishop Bill Hamon.

Parsons Publishing House
P. O. Box 410063
Melbourne, FL 32940 USA
www.ParsonsPublishingHouse.com
Info@ParsonsPublishingHouse.com

Book 1 of The Voices Trilogy by Dr. Robert Gay.

All Scripture quotations, unless otherwise indicated, are taken from the *New King James Version*® (NKJV). Copyright © 1982 by Thomas Nelson, Inc. Used by permission. All rights reserved.

Scripture quotations marked (KJV) are taken from the Holy Bible, King James Version, Cambridge, 1769.

Scripture quotations marked (MKJV) are taken from the Holy Bible, Modern King James Version. Copyright © 1962-1998 by Jay P. Green, Sr. Used by permission of the copyright holder.

Publisher has opted to reference satan and related names with lowercase letters.

Cover Art by Micah Gay.

Copyright © 2021 by Robert Gay.
All rights reserved.
ISBN-13: 978-160273-137-0
ISBN-10: 160273137-3
Library of Congress Control Number: 2021948177
Printed in the United States of America.
For World-Wide Distribution.

DEDICATION

This book is dedicated to all the men and women, prophets and pastors, who have pioneered in the prophetic ministry. Your spiritual labor has helped bring a restoration of spiritual giftings that express the voice of the Lord within the earth.

To those who have strived to maintain a pure word that precisely articulates the heart of God, diligently continue in your zeal for integrity and accuracy. Know that the seeds you have sown will bear good fruit and be rewarded in the days to come.

> Therefore, my beloved brethren, be steadfast, immovable, always abounding in the work of the Lord, knowing that your labor is not in vain in the Lord (1 Corinthians 15:58).

VOICES

TABLE OF CONTENTS

VOICES

FOREWORD

by Bishop Bill Hamon

Bishop of Christian International Apostolic-Global Network

Robert Gay has done a tremendous job of presenting very important truths concerning how to recognize the voices that are in the world. If you grasp the truths concerning how to recognize and respond to the ten to twelve sources of voices that seek to influence our lives, you will move in wisdom and avoid many bad decisions that could negatively affect your life.

I checked closely how Pastor Robert handled the prophetic voice. In exposing the pitfalls and wrong ways of ministering the prophetic, I can truthfully say that Robert handled these delicate issues with wisdom and grace.

When the Prophetic Movement was birthed at our CI Prophetic conference on October 15, 1988, God caught me up in the Spirit, and Jesus came and handed me a baby. He said, "This represents the Company of Prophets I am raising up to help fulfil My end-time purposes. Will you take a fathering role to co-labor with Me in bringing them forth in the purity and maturity I desire?" I said "yes" and have been doing all in my power to make sure those who participate in the Prophetic Movement keep all their 10 M's in proper order: Manhood,

Ministry, Message, Maturity, Marriage, Methods, Manners, Money, Morality and Motive. I wrote three books on the Prophetic and one on the Apostolic. I have a zeal and commitment to seeing the Prophetic progress and function in the wisdom of God and maturity of Jesus Christ, the true Prophet in and for the Church.

Please do more than read through this book. Study it and meditate on the truths until they become a vital part of your wisdom, character, and way of thinking to live successfully.

Bless you, Robert, for taking the time to study out these truths—receiving the revelation and application to help God's people recognize and respond to the right voices that we daily face. This book fulfills the statement of Jesus that you shall know the truth, and truth shall make you free to rightly discern and obey the right voices.

Books by Bishop Bill Hamon: *The Eternal Church; Prophets & Personal Prophecy; Prophets & the Prophetic Movement; Prophets, Pitfalls, & Principles; Apostles, Prophets & the Coming Moves of God; The Day of the Saints; Who Am I & Why Am I Here; The Final Reformation & Great Awaking; 70 Reasons for Speaking in Tongues; How Can These Things Be?; God's Weapons of War;* and *Your Highest Calling.*

INTRODUCTION

It seems today there is no shortage of voices in the world. Everywhere you turn, there are people making proclamations of their insight. We see them on our televisions, hear them on our podcasts and radios, and read them on social media, blogs, and internet posts. It happens every minute of every hour of every day. It is constant.

We hear voices declaring what they believe to be the truth. We hear voices stating what we know to be false. We hear voices pontificating about their superior knowledge in their field of study and application. We hear the talking heads of news broadcasts as they compete for a place in the minds of an audience.

On top of the audible voices we hear, there are the internal voices that we encounter. There are voices we hear speaking to us. As Christians, this should be a normal thing as we commune with the Holy Spirit. However, every part of our human existence has a voice, and at times, they will all compete for a place of leadership. Each voice seeks to be the one that is acknowledged and heeded. It can sometimes be overwhelming if we fail to understand from where they originate and then how to process them.

After all is said, we are left with the responsibility of sorting out all the voices we hear. We must decide which ones will be embraced and which ones will be discarded. We must determine the validity of all voices seeking a place to reside within us. Which ones of these voices are true, and which ones are false? Which ones seek to help us, and which ones aim to harm us? Which ones are legitimate and which ones are illegitimate? We are faced with this dilemma daily, an overwhelming number of voices that must be sorted and filed into different categories.

The Information Age

We live in a time when information abounds. Some have referred to it as the information age. There is knowledge and information that is readily available to us about everything under the sun and beyond. With a few keystrokes on a computer, you can find information about anything your heart desires. Open a browser on a cell phone, and an entire encyclopedia is at your fingertips. It is truly amazing the degree of knowledge that is accessible to us today.

Along with the advent of all our techno-communication advancements, a deluge of false information has also come. It is called disinformation or misinformation. Unfortunately, our newfound technology has created a platform for the proliferation of false and misleading voices. Thus, the very thing that has given us access to an immeasurable knowledge base has also given way for the greatest onslaught of false information ever known to man.

The War of Voices

Humanity is caught in the middle of the war, a battle of truth against lies. We are the ones that determine which narratives will be rejected or believed. We are the ones that determine the winners and the losers. The voices that are believed to be true win out, while the ones we reject lose their footing.

There has always been disagreement between people. Everyone sees things differently from others. My wife, Stacey, and I have been married for 40 years; we are opposites and seem always to observe things differently. Even the things we agree upon are for different reasons.

I recognize there are always two sides to a story, and there is usually some measure of truth contained in both. However, the proliferation of conflicting information, narratives, and stories now seems to be diametrically opposed to one another. Many of these contradictory narratives involve life choices we have to make. Our decisions are based upon which narratives we believe and which ones we deem to be false.

This places all of us in a situation where we must be able to properly discern and distinguish the origins of the voices we are hearing. Questions must be asked, and every voice must be tested and evaluated. No longer can we merely believe something because someone said it. We cannot believe something solely because we read it on social media or heard it on a news broadcast. Even more, we cannot believe something merely because we desire it to be the truth. We also cannot trust a voice to be true just because it says, "The Lord told me."

People cannot discern things properly if they firstly fail to understand their own human makeup and existence. We must understand that we are a spirit, we have a soul, and we live in a body. Every part of our human existence has a voice, and we must be able to distinguish and discern them. The spirit of man is the discernment center and aids in all the sorting of voices. In this book, I will share, in detail, concerning these things.

The Holy Spirit is Here

We must understand that the voice of the Holy Spirit is real and relevant. He speaks to the hearts of believers through various ways and means; most of them are inaudible to the natural ear. However, when someone is spiritually attuned, it rings as clear as a midnight bell. God still speaks today. His voice can be clearly heard when we tune our hearts to His frequency.

Jesus said the Holy Spirit would lead us into all truth. He was not merely speaking of the truth of the Word of God, but the Holy Spirit also reveals to us what is true and false in natural things as our helper and aid. He is here to illuminate the things that are right and the things that are wrong; this is a primary role of the Holy Spirit in the lives of believers. He desires to do this daily, not just speak to us when we are in a church service.

The Holy Spirit is the spirit of truth. The more we handle the truth, the greater we recognize His voice, enabling us to distinguish what is false and misleading. As we familiarize ourselves with the voice of the Holy Spirit, He leads and guides us down the path of life.

We Must Know

I believe more than ever that we must be able to distinguish the voices that we hear. We hear them every day. We hear them everywhere. We must properly discern the voices that we hear. Failure to discern and hear correctly will cause us to go awry; following the wrong voice can be disastrous. Whereas following the right voice will produce life.

There are biblical keys and principles that we can apply within our lives that will help us distinguish the voices that we hear. It will enable us to make the right choices. It will help us make correct decisions.

Listening to the wrong voice will cause a wrong decision. Listening to the right voice will cause a right decision. It is just that simple. The first step in making right choices is the knowledge of different voices and the language they speak. We must know where a voice is originating to determine if we will heed it or not.

In this book, I will discuss the primary voices that every Christian needs to recognize and distinguish. These are foundational stones for the life of a believer. Failure to fully understand these voices can produce confusion in the lives of good people that love God, which can cause them to behave in strange and bizarre manners. However, proper discernment will effectively guide them down the path of life; it will be beneficial and produce great blessing.

The understanding of the voices we hear gives us the ability to do the right thing. It enables us to evaluate things accurately, and we cease walking in the dark. Allow the principles contained in this book to produce spiritual insight so that you can properly discern and distinguish the voices you hear.

VOICES

1

MANY KINDS OF VOICES

> There are, it may be, so many kinds of voices in the world, and none of them is without signification. Therefore, if I know not the meaning of the voice, I shall be unto him that speaketh a barbarian, and he that speaketh shall be a barbarian unto me (1 Corinthians 14:10-11, KJV).

Many years ago, as I was studying this passage of Scripture, the word "voices" stood out. I sensed the Holy Spirit quicken this to me and provoke me to do additional study. I immediately began to do some in-depth research on this entire Scripture passage focusing on the word "voices," and more specifically, "many kinds of voices." This phrase indicates there are numerous voices we hear and encounter.

We live in a day where voices abound; they are everywhere. No matter where we go, voices are being broadcast. Whether on television, social media, news broadcasts, or film, we are constantly bombarded by voices containing numerous opinions, ideologies, doctrines, and philosophies. Some of them are loud, and some are soft. Some of them are appealing, and some are less appealing. Some are sour, and some are sweet. Some are true, and some are false. The reality is there is no shortage of voices today.

The challenge for all of us is to determine the correct ones and the incorrect ones. To which ones do we give our ear, and which ones should we reject? This is not always easy since all these voices are articulated with conviction and justification. Every one of these voices believes they are right. All of them think that they have the latest revelation that will elevate mankind. They all believe implementing the principle or doctrine that they are speaking will be the salvation for all the world.

So, how do we differentiate between voices we are hearing? How do we find their source of origin? How do we successfully navigate through the maze of voices that are being promoted and propagated? Which voice comes from God? What voice is from the devil? What voice is from our natural man and emotions? What voices that we hear, yet are inaudible to others, do we acknowledge and obey? What voices do we reject? These are questions we have all struggled with at some point within our lives. Frankly, it would be unusual not to ask these things.

Every believer should desire to hear correctly. It should be our desire to refrain from being deceived by heeding the wrong voices. Our heart's desire should be to hear and follow the voice of the Lord.

Everything You Hear Is Not True

One of the most important things to understand is that everything you hear is not true. Unfortunately, you will hear more inaccurate information than accurate. More untrue things are floating around than true. Believing everything you hear is foolish; it is a sign of gullibility and ultimately will bring destruction.

Even though something is written in a book, it does not automatically make it true and accurate. Hearing a story on the news does not mean it is valid. Someone posting a cute meme on social media does not mean that you can go to the bank with it. A message from your best friend does not equate to their message being correct. Finally, hearing something in your prayer time does not mean that the Holy Spirit said it.

The first step in hearing correctly is recognizing that the majority of what you hear will not be true, accurate, or valid. Understanding that truth is not being pessimistic; it is the mark of discernment and discretion. It is a mark of maturity that will cause you to avoid many traps the enemy uses to ensnare believers.

Paul specifically said, "There are so many kinds of VOICES in the world." If there are so many, that means that all of them are not correct. Let me give you a simple illustration. A simple math question is asked to 100 different people, "What is two plus two?" To the question, there are 100 different answers submitted. Only one of them has the answer of "four." That means there are 99 wrong answers out of the 100. Do you get the picture? There are 100 different voices attempting to answer the same questions, and all the answers are different. However, only one of them is the correct answer; the rest are wrong or inaccurate.

VOICES

Good Intentions and Accuracy

While good intentions are wonderful, it doesn't make a voice correct or accurate. Someone can possess the greatest intentions in the world, yet their voice can be absolutely wrong. They can have a heart of gold, but that does not make their voice the one that should be heeded. Good intentions do not make a voice accurate or true.

Many times, I have seen people believe what their friend told them solely because of perceived good intentions. They believed that their friend told them "the truth" and was motivated by love. However, motive and love do not make a voice right or accurate.

Honestly, I would rather hear something accurate from someone who had no care for me rather than hear something false from someone who loves me. When making a decision, I don't need consolation; I need accuracy and correctness. Deciding things based solely upon the perception that someone loves or cares for you without factoring in the accuracy and truth of their voice is foolish and unwise. However, many Christians do this on a regular basis resulting in poor decisions.

In relationship to hearing the voice of the Lord, the only thing worse than hearing nothing is the inability to distinguish what you are hearing. This inability can be linked to numerous historical travesties. An entire book could be written about all the people who did awful things in the name of "a voice told me to do it."

Some people were totally controlled by demons and had evil hearts, but there were others led astray by the voices they heard.

Their inability to distinguish the origin of the voice they heard led them down a path of great destruction.

The Inability to Discern Results in Tragedy

There are accounts of dictators and tyrants who committed gross human rights crimes because they heard a voice tell them to do it. Their inability to distinguish the voice led them down a road of war and murder. There are accounts of leaders doing things in the name of "God spoke to me" that harmed many people. When leaders cannot properly distinguish voices, there will be mishaps and problems. They will ultimately make the wrong decision and do the wrong thing.

Cults have been initiated solely because someone heard a voice or had a vision. They believed what they heard was the voice of the Lord, as did those who followed them. However, it proved to be the voice of deception.

A minister by the name of Jim Jones was an ordained minister of a recognized denomination in the United States. Reports are that he heard a voice speak to him to move his ministry to Jonestown, Guyana. In 1978, he ultimately led a mass suicide where 918 people died. This became known as the Jonestown Massacre. All of his followers drank cyanide-laced Flavor Aid™ at their leader's directive. This incident is where the phrase "drink the Kool-Aid" originated.

It is common that cult and false religious leaders heard a voice or saw something supernatural. However, their inability to distinguish where the voice originated led them down a road of demise and destruction. Some of these men were initially Christian pastors and leaders. Yet, mistaking the voice of deception for the voice of the Lord caused them to go awry.

When someone cannot properly distinguish where the voices they hear originate, they will wander into error. This fact not only applies to ministers but to every human being. It does not matter how spiritual someone claims to be; the inability to distinguish the voices they hear will ultimately lead them down the path of destruction.

The Lord Told Me

People do bizarre things today in the name of "the Lord told me." I have witnessed people divorce their spouse, leave their children, and suddenly make unwise geographical moves solely because they heard a voice speak to them. I am confident that God does not appreciate being the scapegoat for the unwise and sinful things people do in His name.

We must continually guard our hearts. The Bible exhorts us to keep it protected because out of it flows the issues of life. Many things can taint our hearing. If we constantly spend time listening to unbiblical and unproven opinions and theories, it will poison our spiritual well. From there, we may hear things that will be mistaken for the voice of the Lord.

As a pastor, people have come into my office and told me that God had spoken for them to do certain things. Some of these things were contrary to Scripture and violated biblical principles, and much of it was unloving. Sometimes these things were sinful in nature and not Christlike. However, they believed they heard the voice of the Lord. I have witnessed pastors and ministers do the same.

It is important to understand that EVERYTHING YOU HEAR IS NOT FROM GOD. We must be able to distinguish (discern) where the voice originates. What has given power to the voice we are hearing? Why are we hearing this, and what do we do with it? All these questions must be accurately addressed, or we will live merely hoping we heed the right voice.

> "Therefore, if I know not the meaning of the voice,
> I shall be unto him that speaketh a barbarian..."
> (1 Corinthians 14:11, KJV).

The apostle Paul said that if we do not know the meaning of the voices we hear, then we will become a barbarian. I recognize that Paul is speaking specifically of tongues in manifestation within the church gathering; however, there is a spiritual principle in this verse of Scripture that we need to understand. When we fail to properly distinguish and discern the voices we hear, we will conduct our lives like barbarians. If we fail to properly distinguish where the voice originates, we will do things that are crazy and bizarre. We will end up saying that God said things He never said.

The Power and Meaning

The Greek word that is translated as "meaning" in this passage of Scripture is *dunamis.* This is a familiar word to most Spirit-filled believers; it is the word that is commonly understood to refer to the supernatural power of God. In this passage, it is not referring exclusively to the power of God but to the point of origination that empowers a voice to be proclaimed or broadcast.

Every voice you hear, in the natural and the spirit, has a source of power. In the natural realm, the news you hear has a power source that is multi-faceted. The power behind these voices is editors, newscasters, advertisers, along with the corporate officers and board members of these companies. All of these things are what gives power to these voices.

Unfortunately, much of the news we hear today is incorrect and laced with fabrications and exaggerations, particularly non-peer-reviewed news agencies. Most all of it is slanted in one direction or the other, which has produced a deluge of false information. These voices require a source from where they receive power to be heard and broadcast.

In the spirit, the source of power for the voice of the Lord is the Holy Spirit. While His voice has power contained in it, we also give it power in our lives as we listen attentively and give ourselves over to it. As we surrender to His will and purpose, we release the power of His voice within our lives.

Things that we feel and experience in life have a voice. The voice of unforgiveness will tell you to separate from the one who hurt you. Sometimes it will even speak in the language of revenge and justification. The voice of anger may encourage someone to do something evil to another.

When someone hears these kinds of voices without properly distinguishing them, they will say they had a sensing or a feeling to respond or act in a particular manner. Most of the time, these actions equate to unholy behavior. Sometimes they will even say...yes, you guessed it, "The Lord told me."

If we do not know that an offense has given power to the voice of unforgiveness, we will mistake it for something else. This will lead to wrong decisions and choices that damage relationships and produce destruction. Let me say it another way: you will act like a spiritual barbarian.

Barbaric Behavior

Paul said that when we do not understand where voices originate or what has given them power, we will become like a barbarian. The word that Paul uses here also means *foreigner.* In other words, one's behavior will become foreign when misunderstanding and misinterpreting the voices they hear. Strange behavior and actions will happen when one fails to accurately distinguish the voices they are hearing.

Barbarians had the reputation of being brutal and cruel. They were known to be unmannerly and narcissistic in their conduct, caring about no one while embodying the very essence of fleshly behavior. Barbarians were always looking for a fight and were insensitive to others.

Interestingly, the term "barbarian" originated from the Greeks who used it to describe those who did not speak or understand their language. These barbarians also followed none of the Greek customs. While the Greeks prided themselves on their civility, barbarians practiced everything but that. While the use and understanding of the word dealt primarily with the failure to understand the Greek language, there was a connection between deficient language competency and unbecoming behavior.

The unfortunate truth is that those who fail to distinguish the voices they hear correctly become barbaric in their actions. We could say it this way: those who fail to recognize the voices they hear correctly will act crazy and do strange, foreign, and bizarre things. When people improperly distinguish the voices they hear, they respond incorrectly. As a result, they usually make wrong choices and wrong decisions, which leads to wrong actions that become justified with the words, "I heard God say."

Passing the Test

One of the things we must understand is that hearing a voice speak to you never justifies an action. Everything must be tested and proven; it must be scrutinized by the spiritual measuring tool of the Bible. Here is a little saying to put to memory:

If it doesn't pass the test, that voice you must arrest.

The idea and thought that came from the voice you heard will have to be discerned as false and illicit if it cannot pass the test. Any voice that speaks anything contrary to what God has already said in His Word must be labeled and judged as illegitimate. It does not mean the voice fails to exist; it merely means you should not obey or follow it.

If someone cannot properly discern the voices they hear, they will act like a spiritual barbarian. They will respond incorrectly. Crazy and bizarre actions will be the result. It will cause them to do things that are not understandable to others. People will scratch their heads in bewilderment as they watch the actions of insanity conducted by those who failed to discern things properly.

No One Is Infallible

It is important to realize that no one is infallible. On more than one occasion, I have heard people say to me, "I know God spoke to me, and nothing can convince me otherwise." The worst thing that anyone can do with respect to hearing the voice of the Lord is to claim infallibility. This is something I was taught by a great spiritual father. Failure to entertain the idea that we can incorrectly hear will assure that we miss it.

Therefore, we must maintain a humble spirit and never be pompous about what we believe God has spoken to us.

Failure to allow what we hear to be judged and evaluated will automatically disqualify it. Those claiming infallibility will ultimately be led down a path of destruction since any counsel that is contrary will be discounted. These kinds of claims of inerrant accuracy represent the pinnacle of pride and arrogance. Remaining meek, pliable, and teachable will prevent us from walking in error. We must allow the voices that we hear to be measured by the Word in precept, principle, and spirit.

When anyone improperly discerns the voices they hear, they will act like a barbarian. They will speak and do things unwisely. More than ever, it is essential for us to properly discern and distinguish the voices we are hearing. Ask the Holy Spirit to sharpen your ability to hear correctly and distinguish voices. Surround yourself with those who will speak honestly and truthfully to you. It will prevent you from becoming a spiritual barbarian.

The Voice of the Shepherd

In my years as a pastor, on more than one occasion, I've had people tell me they heard something from God. Many people heard accurately; however, many did not. In some cases, they severely missed it.

When something was presented to me, and I knew it was inaccurate, I fulfilled my pastoral responsibility to tell them that they heard incorrectly. However, many times, in their ears, my voice sounded like the voice of the stranger rather than the shepherd. They immediately judged the voice of the shepherd that God had placed within their lives as barbaric, controlling, and evil. At the same time, they relished in the thing they heard, which they incorrectly determined to be the voice of the Lord.

Just as Paul said, since they could not properly discern and distinguish the voices they heard, my voice became like a barbarian. Instead of the voice of the shepherd, they heard the voice of a barbarian. Instead of hearing the heart of God, they heard the voice of their own predetermined disposition.

In almost all these situations, these were good people. I do not doubt for a minute that they loved the Lord. I believe they were saved and Spirit-filled. However, the inability to distinguish and discern the voices they heard caused them to reject the voice of the shepherd. Think about it!

We need to understand how deception enters the hearts of good people. No one who is deceived believes they are deceived. They believe they have heard the correct voice and are doing the right thing. They believe they have heard from God. However, they "miss the boat" because they cannot properly distinguish the voices they are hearing. In my upcoming book, I will give some stories elaborating on how these things operate and function.

Edifying of the Church

"Even so ye, forasmuch as ye are zealous of spiritual gifts, seek that ye may excel to the edifying of the church" (1 Corinthians 14:12, KJV).

After Paul speaks of knowing and discerning the voices we hear, he follows up with a directive to seek to excel in edifying the Church. What is he saying? He is declaring that we need to learn to distinguish the voices we hear so we can help build the Church.

The Greek word translated "edifying" means to build a dwelling. It also refers to the architecture within a plan to establish a structure. If what we are hearing is not pointing to edify the Church, then we must consider it an illegitimate voice regardless of how convinced we are of its accuracy.

Please hear this: **if you are hearing things that fail to help build up the Church, then you are not hearing the voice of the Lord.** Period! Hearing correctly will result in the Church being built up and made strong. Properly distinguishing the voices that you hear will help build and strengthen the local church. Voices that make their goal to destroy local churches, their leaders, or members are not the voice of the Lord. That is the voice of the enemy!

When believers fail to properly discern the voices they hear, they fail to edify the Church. They do bizarre things and bring reproach to the body of Christ. They end up tearing down rather than building up. They end up saying things that hurt other believers in the name of "the Lord told me." They prophesy bizarre things and bring confusion. These are things that must be changed.

The first principle in edifying the Church involves properly discerning and identifying the voices you are hearing. Failure to do so will result in reproach being brought upon the body of Christ, and those within the Church will be hurt needlessly.

Knowing the origin of the voice you are hearing is imperative in the life of a believer. Properly distinguishing and discerning the voices that we hear will result in the eradication of spiritually bizarre behavior. It will cause the Church to be edified, and thus it will be made strong.

My prayer is that you will allow the revelation of the Holy Spirit to resound in your spirit. I pray, like the apostle Paul, that the eyes of your understanding will be enlightened. May our ears become sensitive and our hearts wise to discern the voices that we hear.

Father God, help us today to correctly distinguish the voices that we hear. In the name of Jesus, I pray. Amen.

2

THE SPIRIT—
HUB OF SPIRITUAL EXISTENCE

> Now may the God of peace Himself sanctify
> you completely; and may your whole spirit,
> soul, and body be preserved blameless at the
> coming of our Lord Jesus Christ (1
> Thessalonians 5:23).

One of the first things we must grasp to properly distinguish
the voices we hear is to understand our human existence and
makeup. The apostle Paul clearly articulates what this is in the
above verse of Scripture. He prays that God will sanctify you
completely–spirit, soul, and body. We can see from this that
man consists of three separate individual parts. Please put this
to memory: I am a spirit, I have a soul, and I live in a body.

Humanistic teaching says that you are nothing more than the
physiological makeup of your body, which means you are a
body with a brain. All aspects of the spirit of man are ignored.
If it cannot be seen with the eye or touched with the hand, then
it does not exist in scientific philosophy. However, the spirit
of man is the most important and primary part of man's
existence.

You Are a Spirit

In this verse, Paul mentions the spirit of man first. Why does he do that? It is because the spirit of man is the real you. It is the part that will live eternally and never cease to exist. It is the part of you that makes you more than a zombie walking on the planet. It is the part of you from which flows the true issues of life. Life does not flow from your body and brain alone; it flows from your spirit man.

The spirit of man is the part of you that is made a new creation at the time of salvation, not your soul or body (2 Corinthians 5:17). It is the container of eternal life. It is the part of you that becomes the righteousness of God in Christ Jesus (2 Corinthians 5:21). Your spirit is the part of you where the Holy Spirit makes His dwelling place.

It is the spirit of man that possesses the ability to connect to the spiritual realm. It is the spirit of man which enables us to hear voices in that realm. It is the spirit of man that can hear the voice of the Holy Spirit. The spirit of man is the command center for spiritual existence.

Created to Hear

As a spirit being, you are created to hear voices that cannot be heard in the natural realm. This is specifically true for those who are born again since their spirit man has been made alive unto God. You were once dead in trespasses and sin, but now you are alive. Your spirit man is alive and now can hear and distinguish voices. People who are unsaved can also hear some of these voices but cannot discern them by the Spirit.

We should not think it strange that we can hear voices. While many believe someone is insane or lost their mind if they say they heard a voice speak to them, it should be the norm for Spirit-filled believers. It is not bizarre, strange, or weird. It is the way that God created us to operate and function in the earth.

As spirit beings, we were made to hear voices that are not heard in the natural realm. It is not an odd abnormality to hear these voices; however, we must be able to identify their place of origin. It is only by the Spirit that we can do that.

> But God has revealed them to us through His Spirit. For the Spirit searches all things, yes, the deep things of God. For what man knows the things of a man except the spirit of the man which is in him? Even so no one knows the things of God except the Spirit of God. Now we have received, not the spirit of the world, but the Spirit who is from God, that we might know the things that have been freely given to us by God. These things we also speak, not in words which man's wisdom teaches but which the Holy Spirit teaches, comparing spiritual things with spiritual. But the natural man does not receive the things of the Spirit of God, for they are foolishness to him; nor can he know them, because they are spiritually discerned (1 Corinthians 2:10-14).

Notice in this passage of Scripture that Paul specifically talks about knowing. Paul emphasizes the truth that there are things that God desires us to know. While there are many principles that can be derived from this passage, I want to focus on the point that God wants you to have knowledge about the spirit realm. It is the redeemed spirit of man that can perceive and receive this knowledge by properly discerning voices.

Seeing and Discerning

The Greek word that is translated "know" means to see and discern. Paul said man's way of seeing and discerning is through his spirit. It is the spirit of man that possesses the ability to see, discern, and distinguish the voices that are heard. Voices are not distinguished through the soul or body of man; they are discerned through the spirit of man that is aided by the Holy Spirit.

Paul said that the natural man cannot receive the things of the spirit. This is very important to understand. There is only one part of you, your spirit man, that possesses the ability to receive, understand, and discern the things of the spirit realm. Your body and soul cannot do that. They have a different purpose that God created them to fulfill. It is a foundational principle in properly discerning the voices you hear to know that your spirit is the discernment center.

Voices that you hear cannot be discerned through a feeling you experience within your body. Regardless of a "chill bump" or "electrical charge" you feel, it is not the measuring tool for the things of the Spirit. Only one part of your trichotomy can distinguish the voices that you hear; that is your spirit man. Before you go any further in this book, this principle must be grasped and understood: **Feelings, emotions, and sensations have absolutely nothing to do with discerning and distinguishing the voices that we hear.**

The Recreated Spirit of Man

When someone is born again, the very nature of God is received in their spirit. The old man that was dead becomes alive. That means what you could not hear before salvation now becomes perceivable. What was foreign and strange yesterday now becomes the norm for you as a recreated spirit being. You were once dead and could not hear a spiritual shout, but now you are alive and can hear the slightest whisper of the Holy Spirit.

Since your spirit man is alive, it has a voice. Living things have a voice. Every living thing that God created has a voice. Animals have a voice. Even a tree will emit sounds when blown by strong winds (though we are not promoting carrying on a dialogue with vegetation). Living things make sounds and have a voice.

The real you, your spirit man, speaks a language. Not only does it speak and have a voice, but it is made to understand, recognize, and distinguish voices. One of the primary functions of our spirit man is to distinguish and discern things we hear in the natural and spiritual. Your spirit man is created to be the hub of spiritual understanding and discernment. It acts as a spiritual filter to hold on to what is legitimate while refusing what is erroneous.

> "The spirit of a man is the lamp of the LORD,
> Searching all the inner depths of his heart"
> (Proverbs 20:27).

It is the spirit of man that God uses to illuminate things within our lives. God does not use the soul or the body; He utilizes the spirit of man. It shines the light in dark places. It illuminates the path that we are to take within our lives. The recreated spirit of man has a knowing of what is right and wrong, good and bad, holy and unholy. It will lead us in the right direction if we tune our ears to hear and listen.

The Holy Spirit communicates with your spirit man, not your soul or body. Our spirit is the hub of our spiritual hearing; it is our spiritual communication center. Everything that God does in our lives originates within the spirit of man.

As was stated previously, every living thing has a voice. Your spirit man has a voice. The real you speaks a language. Your redeemed spirit will say things that agree with the will and purpose of God because that is where the Holy Spirit dwells. The Holy Spirit does not live in your soul and body; He lives and dwells in your spirit. Our bodies are the temple of the Holy Spirit solely because it houses our spirit man.

Clarity Does Not Determine Correctness

Many times, people hear things that come from the voice of the soul and think it is their spirit or the Holy Spirit. However, we must learn the difference. The volume of the voice that you hear never determines where it originates. When a voice shouts, it means nothing about its place of origin; neither when a voice whispers does it determine from where it comes.

When people hear something clearly, they will sometimes think that it is the voice of the Lord. However, clarity in a voice does not determine where it originates. I've heard voices very clearly before that when tested were determined to be illegitimate. The clarity of a voice does not determine the correctness of a voice.

Even an angelic visitation does not mean that it is from the Lord. The apostle Paul said that if an angel appeared and spoke anything contrary to what he was preaching, let him be accursed, which means it would be judged as an illegitimate voice.

The power of a voice does not determine its accuracy or legitimacy. The sensationalism of a voice does not determine its legitimacy. The physical manifestation produced by a voice does not determine its legitimacy. The legitimacy of a voice will be primarily determined by three things that we will discuss later, the witness of your spirit, the voice of the Holy Spirit, and the written Word of God. However, it is essential first to realize that hearing a voice concisely and clearly does not necessarily indicate it is the voice of the Lord.

Let Your Conscience Be Your Guide

> For when Gentiles, who do not have the law, by nature do the things in the law, these, although not having the law, are a law to themselves, who show the work of the law written in their hearts, their conscience also bearing witness, and between themselves their thoughts accusing or else excusing them (Romans 2:14-15).

I'm sure you have heard the old saying, "Let your conscience be your guide." It is actually more than a nice thought; it is a truth that we should practice.

For a Christian, the conscience of man is the voice from the spirit of man. It is the voice of conviction that is inside of us.

Traditionally, conscience has been considered a part of the soul, specifically your mind, that has some sort of knowledge of right and wrong. However, biblically the conscience of the believer is found in the spirit of man.

While there has been debate as to the actual place the conscience is located, I do not believe it would be beneficial to discuss it in this writing. If it were in the soul of man, its function is still the same. So, we will not debate its place but agree on its purpose.

This passage of Scripture states that the conscience bears witness, which means that conscience has a voice. It is the still small voice that gives us a sense of right and wrong. It will give us a "green light" when we are moving in the right direction. It will provide us with a "red light" if we move in the wrong direction. It will prick our hearts if we start to do the wrong thing. The conscience of man is the voice that keeps us from entering the danger zone.

Once we are born again, the law of God is written upon our hearts. Our conscience will bear witness (speak in agreement) with that law. The voice of conscience will always agree with the law of God. The conscience does not speak outside the boundaries of what God has already spoken. It functions harmoniously with the recreated spirit of man that is alive unto God.

The Inward Sensing and Knowing

Often, the conscience will not manifest as a voice that is heard, rather as an inward sensing or knowing. It will produce a spiritual sense of peace and tranquility if what you are doing is right and correct. It will produce a spiritual sense of uneasiness if what you are contemplating is wrong. The sense of peace means that there is nothing that violates your conscience. The sense of uneasiness means that you should not proceed.

Many believers fail to realize that violating the voice of conscience is sinful behavior. To override one's conscience is a sign of self-will and stubbornness. God placed the voice of conscience on the inside of us to illuminate our path and prevent us from walking in the wrong direction. It lets us know the correct way and if there is danger on the horizon.

> Now when much time had been spent, and sailing was now dangerous because the Fast was already over, Paul advised them, saying, "Men, I perceive that this voyage will end with disaster and much loss, not only of the cargo and ship, but also our lives." Nevertheless, the centurion was more persuaded by the helmsman and the owner of the ship than by the things spoken by Paul (Acts 27:9-11).

The apostle Paul was being transported by ship while in captivity. He told the centurion in charge that he perceived that the voyage would end in disaster. The word translated "perceive" means to discern and observe. Paul did not say that the Lord spoke to him, or an angel of the Lord appeared to him; he merely said that he perceived that it was unwise to set sail.

Paul's sensing was that of his spirit man—the voice of the inward witness. There was an uneasiness that existed within him that brought about a warning to those in charge. No scrolls were unfurled from heaven, no lightning was seen, nor thunder heard; it was merely a sense of uneasiness.

Unfortunately, the centurion listened to the wrong voice. Rather than heed the warning from Paul, he listened to the helmsman and owner of the ship. That was a bad mistake on his part. He set sail, and the entire ship broke apart at sea, losing all its cargo. God protected all those onboard, but only because Paul was on the ship. Failure to heed what Paul was sensing in his spirit cost them the entire vessel and all its contents. This reveals the high cost of ignoring the sensing of our spirit man and overriding the still small voice.

The mistakes that I've made in my life can be traced back to violating the still small voice. My conscience was saying, "This is the wrong way." However, I decided that I would pull a Frank Sinatra and do it my way. Those choices and decisions did not end up with a positive outcome. Fortunately, much of the results were minimized because I quickly turned around.

Loss is always suffered when we fail to heed the voice of conscience. While God can often restore the loss, we needlessly go through pain when we willfully violate our conscience and act on our predisposed opinions. Bottom line, if you don't have peace about it, don't do it!

Follow Peace

The language of the conscience of man is peace. When peace is present, that is its voice telling us to proceed. When peace is absent, that is its voice telling us to stop. We must learn to "follow after the things that make peace" (Romans 14:19). Go after that which produces peace and fulfillment. Avoid that which produces a sense of uneasiness.

It is important that we understand that everyone's conscience will not function the same. Therefore, there are things that your conscience will not allow you to do that may be acceptable for others. Destruction would be the result if you were to do it, while others may have no negative effects within their lives if they were to do the same. Some things are not explicitly declared in the Bible to be sinful. For these things, we are to be led by the voice of conscience.

We should never try to force our conscience on others, whether we feel it is right or wrong. Neither should we do something that violates our conscience just because someone else believes it is permissible. If there is a biblical reason and justification for what you believe the voice of conscience is saying, then you can proclaim it. However, if it is not clearly defined as right or wrong, leave it to the conscience of others to determine what they will do.

Whatever we do, we should do it in faith. We should do it with confidence and assurance. We should not be wondering if it is right or wrong. If you fail to have a sense of peace about something, then you cannot do it in good conscience. So, just don't do it!

Red Light Means Stop

In the mid-1990s, I was presented with a ministry opportunity to move out west to become part of a dynamic local church. I had numerous opportunities to minister there and was very excited about the prospects of moving our family and becoming a part of their ministry. It seemed in the natural like the perfect situation that would allow us to further what God had called us to accomplish.

My wife, Stacey, traveled with me to meet the pastor and his wife several times. They were wonderful people, and we had great fellowship with them. Things were shaping up for us to move there. Everything seemed to fit together perfectly.

One weekend we flew out to look at homes in the area. As we were making some of our final preparations, my wife looked at me and said, "This isn't the Lord; I can't get peace about this." I was shocked and displeased at what I heard. We discussed it at length and had a fevered debate. My position was that this was a deal we could not refuse. Her position was that she could not go there in good conscience.

She had no objection to anyone who was there in the church. She loved the area and the people. However, she could never get a peaceful sensing about moving there. So, we finally resolved to remain in Panama City, Florida.

A year later, because of some things that a man within their church did, that church collapsed. It was no fault of the pastor other than he trusted someone who proved to be untrustworthy. Unfortunately, this caused many people to be hurt and caused animosity to grow until the church was not sustainable.

If we had proceeded with moving, we would have been caught in the crossfire. There could have been great loss for us because of this volatile situation.

My wife never said that the Lord told her, "Don't go." She merely had an uneasiness about us moving, a check in her spirit. It was the same thing that happened to the apostle Paul when he perceived danger was ahead if they sailed on their voyage. My wife sensed problems if we moved. I'm glad we heeded the still small voice within her spirit; it protected us from potential loss.

Sons Are Led by the Spirit

> For as many as are led by the Spirit of God, these are sons of God. For you did not receive the spirit of bondage again to fear, but you received the Spirit of adoption by whom we cry out, "Abba, Father." The Spirit Himself bears witness with our spirit that we are children of God (Romans 8:14-16).

It is the reality of being sons of God that gives us the ability to be led by the Spirit of the Lord. When we become a new creation in Christ, our spirit man is resurrected, which gives us the ability to hear the voice of the Holy Spirit. You see, a dead man cannot hear; only a living being has the capability of hearing. We possess the ability to be led by the Spirit because we are sons and daughters of God with His Spirit dwelling within us. We are alive unto God and can now hear the voice of the Lord.

One of the characteristics of sons and daughters of God is this ability to be led by the Holy Spirit. It is a distinguishing mark that declares we are a part of the family of God. People who do not belong to the family of God lack this ability to be led. Instead, they wander. Just like the children of Israel in the wilderness, they wander around with no internal guidance. They have no spiritual compass for their lives.

The Israelites in the wilderness depended on a cloud by day and a fire by night to show them the way. It is interesting to note that they were dependent on external things for direction. They were not born of the Spirit because that experience was unavailable. So, they depended on a cloud and a fire to lead them. Depending on external things to give us direction indicates that we are not operating as sons, rather spiritual vagabonds. You were not designed to live in that manner; you are a child of God.

As born-again believers, we are not wilderness-walkers. Our spirit man, aided by the Holy Spirit, illuminates the path before us. God reveals to us the right and wrong direction. We are not the children of darkness; we are children of the light. The Spirit can lead us because we are sons and daughters of God.

Not Forced, but Led

The previous verses of Scripture tell us that we did not receive a spirit of bondage. Paul was declaring that we were not made to be slaves. God designed for us to be led, not forced. Being led requires voluntary submission to His voice, not mandatory enslavement. God never forces us to do anything. He does not force us to heed His voice. Instead, He instructs us to willingly submit so that we can receive the blessing it brings—the blessing of sonship.

A slave may receive a wage, but only sons receive an inheritance. When we fail to be led by the Spirit, we take the position of a slave. I desire to receive an inheritance, not merely a paycheck. Wages are based on work and performance, whereas inheritance is based upon a relationship as a son. When we heed the voice of the Spirit, we position ourselves as sons and daughters of God to receive our inheritance from the Lord.

Could it be that some believers fail to receive their spiritual inheritance in Christ because they choose to ignore the leading of His Spirit? Could it be that many Christians forfeit much of what God desires to release in their lives because they follow the wrong voices and lack discernment? Think about it!

It is important for us to understand that the voice of our spirit man will not force us to do anything. There is a peace that comes when we heed the voice of our spirit. However, there is usually a sense of unrest when one chooses to refuse to submit. We must understand the importance of submission if we are going to conduct ourselves as sons of God and be led by the Spirit.

In this passage from Romans, Paul goes on to say we should have no fear where the voice of the Lord will lead us. Again, as many as are led (listen) by the Spirit are sons. This means you have not received a spirit that will lead you to captivity, so you need not fear (my paraphrase). Paul is declaring that you can have confidence that wherever you are led will be a place of peace and safety.

This truth reminds me of Psalm 23. The Lord is my Shepherd... He LEADS me by still waters... He LEADS me in the paths of righteousness. Listening to the voice of your spirit man will cause you to drink from still waters—the river of peace. Being led by the voice of the Spirit will guide you in paths of righteousness, which means you will do the right thing. You will not fall into sin when you are led by the right voice—the voice of your spirit.

Harmonious Operation

The last thing I want you to clearly see in the previous verses of Scripture is that there is a harmonious operation between the Holy Spirit and our redeemed spirit man. They are not at odds with each other. They work cohesively together to the point that it is difficult to distinguish them from each other. We will later discuss the voice of the Holy Spirit, and this truth will become more apparent.

Paul said that the Holy Spirit bears witness with our spirit. "Bears witness" means to speak, say, and declare. So, this means that our spirit man and the Holy Spirit will say the same things. One is not saying one thing while the other is saying something opposite. Your recreated spirit man and the Holy Spirit are on the same page. They function in harmony with one another.

As was said previously, your spirit man is the discernment center. It has a divine ability to discern and distinguish voices that you hear. The primary reason for this is because it is the place where the Holy Spirit takes up residence in the believer. Your spirit is married to the Holy Spirit upon salvation, which gives you the ability to listen and hear correctly and distinguish the many voices in the world today.

Your spirit man will confirm the voice of the Holy Spirit and vice versa. This is the reason that prophetic words will often confirm things we have already heard or sensed; the Holy Spirit is bearing witness with our spirit. In prophecy, the Spirit of the

Lord often speaks the same thing we have heard in our times of prayer and seeking the face of God.

God Is Consistent

We must understand that God does not possess split personalities. He is not confused. He is not saying one thing today and then another tomorrow. He does not contradict Himself. Our God is consistent. He is the same yesterday, today, and forever; He never changes. Therefore, His voice does not change.

For a believer, the voice of your spirit man works in conjunction with the voice of the Holy Spirit. The spirit of man is the candle of the Lord. God uses our redeemed spirit to bring illumination and insight. Our spirit man is the light that God uses to illuminate and reveal His will and purpose for our lives. When we follow the still small voice, we move in His direction.

One with the Holy Spirit

Paul said that he who is joined to the Lord is one spirit (1 Corinthians 6:17). This means that your redeemed spirit man and the Holy Spirit are inseparable. They speak the same language. They say the same things. When you hear one, you hear the other.

My wife, Stacey, and I have been married for over 40 years. She knows me, and I know her. We have been together for so long that I know what she likes and dislikes. I know what she wants when we go to a restaurant before she sits down. I know her routine every morning, and she knows mine.

Because we have been together for so long and are inseparable, she can speak for me, and I can speak for her. The reason for this is I know how she thinks, and she knows how I think. If I needed someone to go somewhere in my stead, she would be the most accurate representation of me. Even though my children would come very close, she knows me better than anyone else.

As it is in the natural, so it is in the spirit. No one knows your spirit more than the Holy Spirit. You are one; you are united. The Holy Spirit and your spirit man speak the same thing. When we listen to the still small voice, it will bring about God's blessing. The voice of your spirit is the light of the Lord showing you the path of life.

Your spirit man and the Holy Spirit are inseparable. They commune and function together in perfect harmony. What Adam lost at the fall of man in communion and fellowship, Jesus restored through His sacrificial offering. He made a way that your spirit could be united eternally with the Holy Spirit.

Your spirit man has now become the spiritual communication hub within your life. It is now the spiritual discernment center of your personage. You are one with the Holy Spirit, and He is with you. You are a son and can now be led by the Spirit.

3

THE SOUL— HUB OF HUMAN EXISTENCE

> For the word of God is living and powerful,
> and sharper than any two-edged sword,
> piercing even to the division of soul and spirit,
> and of joints and marrow, and is a discerner of
> the thoughts and intents of the heart
> (Hebrews 4:12).

> Therefore lay aside all filthiness and overflow
> of wickedness, and receive with meekness the
> implanted word, which is able to save your
> souls (James 1:21).

The soul of man has often been confused with the spirit of man. In modern Christianity, we talk about "souls saved" when referring to people coming to know the Lord. While there is an element of truth in that statement, the whole truth is the only part of one's trichotomy that is fully transformed at the time of salvation is their spirit man.

The soul itself is in a continuous process of being saved. The soul is saved and delivered through the renewing of the mind and biblical principles that are learned and practiced. The soul is not fully saved at the time of salvation. The salvation of the soul begins at the moment of regeneration but is not fully accomplished at that time. This ongoing process is referred to as sanctification.

The above passage of Scripture found in Hebrews declares it is only by the Word of God that the spirit, soul, and body can be separated and discerned. The way that we can distinguish between what is from the spirit or soul is by the Word. So, we must go to the Bible to clearly define and distinguish the voice of the soul.

The Soul: Intellect, Will, and Emotions

Your soul is comprised of three things: intellect, will, and emotions. Each part of your soul has a unique function. Each part of your soul has its own voice.

The intellect has a voice. It will speak of knowledge it has acquired and is the center of your reasoning capability. Most all human reasoning is the voice of your intellect which is contained within your soul. Human reasoning is the systematic evaluation of facts and information that draws an informed conclusion. It is the center for the logical expression of your human existence. Intellect and reasoning are wonderful, but they are to be subservient to the spirit of man.

Your will is the part of you that makes decisions and then executes them. The will connects the soul to the spirit and the body. Things that we do by the spirit and with our body are activated through an act of the will of man. So, the will is the connective part of you that allows things to operate and function congruently.

Emotions are the part of you that feels things. It is probably the part of your being that makes you human more than anything else. Our emotions can energize us for purpose when channeled the correct way. They also can steer our ship in the wrong direction if left unchecked. Since we were created in the image of God, we realize that God has emotions.

The emotions of man will usually have the loudest voice because it is the center for feelings. If you are upset, the voice of emotions will shout. If you are offended, the voice of emotions will say things that can lead you in the wrong direction. If you feel acceptance, the voice of emotions will sing a love song about the person who accepts you. While emotions are what cause us to be humans with feelings, they can be the most deceptive part of the soul if allowed to be the controlling voice of our lives. The emotions of man must be subservient to the spirit of man along with the intellect and will.

The Voice of Intellect

The soul of man is capable of being programmed by information. Your intellect is formed by the knowledge acquired through study and life experiences. Human logic and reasoning are developed through the processing and application of the information that we have acquired. These things are very important capabilities that God has instilled within us. Without them, it would be impossible to function properly as human beings.

The voice of intellect will primarily regurgitate its knowledge base. Whatever has been deposited there will be the tone of voice that it speaks. This voice responds to one thing, programmed knowledge. It doesn't have the ability to sense things spiritually; it can only articulate information. Nonetheless, it still has a voice. It is the voice of natural knowledge.

The intellect is the mental computer that stores the information it is given. Its purpose is to provide access to that information when it is needed. It functions just like a computer and can do nothing more than what it is programmed to do. When its database is pure and uncorrupted, it can provide unadulterated information for correct natural decisions to be made. The voice of the intellect speaks this information to the other parts of our being so that they can all operate harmoniously.

The voice of the intellect will speak according to its programming, whether it be good or bad. Intellect does not have a conscience; its only purpose is to store and then export information. Your intellect does not have morals. The only morality your intellect receives is what is programmed through learning and what is embraced when the conscience speaks.

Programming the Intellect

The reality is that we spend a lot of our lives programming our intellect. A tremendous amount of time and energy is expended and devoted to this part of our soul. Most children will spend thirteen years in grade school. Many will continue that data deposit in colleges and universities for another two to eight years. This continual data collection can simultaneously begin to affect our conscience, either for good or bad.

Not only do we program our intellect through schools and universities, but also through media. As a result, television and the internet now play a major role in the ongoing development of our intellectual being. The average adult spends right at six hours a day on the internet in some form or another ("Mary Meeker's 2018 Internet Trends").

We live in the information age where knowledge abounds. Unfortunately, some of the knowledge that is acquired through the intellect is not godly knowledge. Much of it is contrary to what God's Word declares because the culture at large is headed in the wrong direction.

The only way that this infusion of ungodly data can be confronted is through the renewing of the mind. In other words, we flush out the incorrect data with the downloads of heaven, that being the Word of God. We will discuss this later in more detail.

The Voice of Human Reasoning

Once information is within man's intellect, human reasoning has a base from which to work and operate. Human reason has a voice that is determined by many factors, with its primary contributor being the intellect. Human reasoning will pull from information contained within the intellect to make what it considers rational decisions. It will then speak in the language of logic and rationale.

Most of the time, human reason will only speak what is sensible given the data and factors of the moment. However, when emotions run high and begin to shout, logical reasoning can be influenced and overcome by the volume of that voice. It will bring some sort of rationale and justification as to why the voice of emotion should be heeded. The voice of reason will then select choice bits of information to justify heeding the voice of emotions.

> I beseech you therefore, brethren, by the mercies of God, that you present your bodies a living sacrifice, holy, acceptable to God, which is your reasonable service. And do not be conformed to this world, but be transformed by the renewing of your mind, that you may prove what is that good and acceptable and perfect will of God (Romans 12:1-2).

It's amazing how much the Bible says concerning our minds, that being our intellect and reasoning faculties. In the above passage of Scripture, the body and mind are both mentioned. These entities of your human makeup can be programmed. The voices of your mind and body can be transformed through the power of the influence of God's Word.

Paul declared that we are not to be conformed to this world. We are not to think (acts of the mind, intellect, and reason) like the world. We are not to behave (acts of the body influenced through carnal desires and thinking) like the world. He specifically indicates that the mind and body left to itself will conform to the environment and culture. The mind and body will both adapt to their surroundings and then emulate what is witnessed. They are programmed by information and then respond accordingly.

This natural cycle is broken and reversed by the transformational process called renewing the mind, which is accomplished by reprogramming the natural man with God's Word. It is the truth God has proclaimed that can transform our thinking and behavior. It changes us from the inside out.

Divine Metamorphosis

The word "transformed" used in the previous Scripture is derived from the Greek word *metamorphoo*. From this, we derive the English word "metamorphosis," which is the same word used to describe the process whereby a caterpillar becomes a butterfly.

If you consider this metamorphic process that happens to a caterpillar, you can see a parallel that can and should take place within our own lives. A caterpillar spins a cocoon that insulates it from the outside world while a transformation occurs inside this protected environment. The change cannot happen outside the cocoon; it happens while the caterpillar is hidden away inside this protective shell.

For us to experience God's transformation within our minds, we must insulate ourselves from worldly thinking and clothe ourselves with the cocoon of His Word. This causes a change in our thinking. Every aspect of our mind is influenced through the saturation and covering of the Word of God, which affects all aspects of our soul: mind, will, intellect, and emotions. Ultimately, this causes a change in the way we behave and act.

Correct Programming

Many believers today program themselves with the wrong information. When the programing has errors, thinking and behavior will have errors too. Today most Christians spend hours on social media and watching television while they are being programmed by broadcast entertainment or the latest news from talking heads. As a result, they become conformed to the world with their thinking and reasoning faculties taking on the nature of the world rather than the nature of God. It becomes error in and error out.

It is important to understand that whatever we consume mentally will be regurgitated through a voice. Thought patterns are produced through what you consume through the eye and ear gates. That's the reason Paul said that faith comes by hearing. Whatever you hear and watch repeatedly will be what you believe regardless of whether it is true or not.

Jesus told His disciples to beware of the leaven of the scribes and Pharisees. He also told them to be careful what you hear. Jesus taught His disciples to guard the programming of their minds. He told them they should beware of things that would cause improper thinking patterns, contradicting what He was teaching them.

The voices we hear that program our minds will give power to the voices contained in our souls. The voices of your soul (intellect, reason, and emotions) will echo what it hears. If we program our minds with negativity, the voices of the soul will be negative. If we program our minds with social media, the voice of your soul will be what your friends are posting and saying. If we program our minds with the Bible, the voices of the soul will be the Word of God. It is just that simple.

For the voices of our souls to be correct, they must be programmed correctly. Your thinking must be transformed so that its voice will speak the right thing. Our minds must experience a metamorphosis through the power of God's Word. If we are going to watch and listen to the news, then we must equally meditate in the Word of God and spending time in prayer and communion with Him. This is the way that our minds and hearts are renewed.

The Will of Man

One of the amazing things about human existence is that we are free moral agents. God gave us the power to choose and make decisions; He gave us a free will. God did not make us robots. No one can force us to do anything; we must choose to do it. While people can be manipulated into doing things through enticement or pain, we still must choose to do it.

The will of man is the decision-making center within your being. Your will determines what you do, say, and carry out in every realm of your life. The will determines what you do in your spirit, soul, and body. I believe that the will of man is the connective aspect of our human existence.

Your will has a voice. The motivation of the will is the desire of man. Whatever man desires is what he usually wills to do. We are generally not willing to do things that we don't desire. Therefore, the will of man must also be programmed so that it desires what God desires.

Ask yourself this question. Would I be reading this book if I did not desire to do so? I am sure the answer to that question would be "no." The sole reason you are reading this writing is because you desire to do it. The strongest thing that influences the will of man is desire. Therefore, the best way to do the right things in our lives is to possess the correct desires and longings.

"I delight to do Your will, O my God,
And Your law is within my heart"
(Psalm 40:8).

The Psalmist said that he delighted to do the will of God. The word translated as "delight" means to desire, to be pleased, or to incline. So, he was declaring that he desired and possessed an inclination to do God's will. The desire he held moved him to do things in agreement with the plan of God. Again, I want to emphasize the importance of desire and its influence on the will of man.

In this verse, he went on to give us insight as to what produced that desire within him. He said, "Your law is within my heart." The Psalmist was declaring that the Word of God was the motivating factor of his personal will, his desire. The Word that was deposited inside his heart produced a desire to do the will of God. That desire then caused him to will to do the correct thing.

We must program our desire with God's Word. As we do, our will responds accordingly. We choose with our will to do the purpose of God. We choose to do the commands and precepts of the Lord because our desire has been changed from a fleshly desire to a spiritual desire. We delight to do the will of God.

The will of man has a voice. It chooses and then tells your spirit, soul, and body what to do. It has the power to choose what you do. The predominant information and programming in your life will determine the voice of your will, which affects the decisions you make.

The Referee Called "Will"

The will of man acts as a referee. It determines what will be done and decisions made based upon factors that surround you. It chooses what voice to act upon when many are screaming. Let me give you a quick example: Someone is faced with a decision concerning a job opportunity. He is a leader in his local church body, and his family is heavily involved there. Thus, they have a place of belonging. The offer he is given is one that doubles his salary; however, he will be required to move to an area where the cost of living is slightly higher. It is also an area where there is no church like the one in which they are involved.

The family will be required to uproot and move to a strange land. The spiritual support system they have grown to love and appreciate will not be present in the new place. Their extended family will be left behind.

The Dilemma of Clutter

As you can see from this example, there is a dilemma. There are many voices that will be competing for a place. The voice of intellect as it relates to financial benefit will be saying, "Yes!" The voice of reason and logic will be weighing all the factors of reward and consequence. It will say, "Yes, but there is this to consider." The voice of emotion will be varied according to the day of the week. One day it may be screaming with excitement from the financial offer. Another day, it may be anxious and apprehensive because of the personal relationship connections that will be lost.

Then there is the voice of the spirit man that seeks to know God's will and purpose. It is what we refer to many times as how we feel about something. Do we sense a "green light" to go or a "red light" to remain? All these voices begin to speak to us, and a decision has to be made.

Sometimes, the clutter of voices makes it difficult to decide. Again, the will of man becomes the central hub of decision-making. The will of man decides to which voice it will give weight. Man's will has the power to either allow the spirit of man to take ascendency or allow a different voice to dominate.

The spirit of man should be the voice that we heed. The voice of our spirit coupled with the voice of the Holy Spirit is the most accurate indicator of what we should do, where we should go, and when we should do it. All major decisions in our lives should primarily be determined by the voice of our spirit.

The Will: The Responsible Party

The will of man is responsible for just about every aspect of our human existence. Your will is a sorting center for all the voices that you hear. Once it decides what voice it will heed, it makes decisions and actions accordingly. Besides the body's involuntary functions, everything we do engages our will. Even sleeping and dreaming are controlled by your will to a certain degree. This is the reason the will of man must be transformed, or it will result in us making wrong choices.

I have personally concluded that the will of man is responsible for believing. Your spirit man cannot believe without your will being involved. Man's will must engage before the spirit of man can do anything. The spirit of man cannot believe by itself. The will of man is like the trigger on a gun; it initiates things to be released. You must choose to believe before faith can be released. However, when we choose to believe, faith is activated, and miracles happen.

> When He had come down from the mountain, great crowds followed him. And behold, a leper came and worshiped him, saying, Lord, if You will, You can make me clean. And Jesus put out His hand and touched him, saying, I will; be clean! And immediately his leprosy was cleansed (Matthew 8:1-3, MKJV).

Please take note of what the leper said to Jesus. He said, "Lord, if you WILL, You can make me clean." Jesus replied by saying, "I WILL; be clean."

The word translated "will" in this passage of Scripture means to determine or resolve. I've concluded that the word "willing" does not merely mean to permit something; I believe it means to choose or decide. Jesus was not saying that He would passively allow healing to happen. He was declaring that He had it within His resolve and was actively choosing to make the man whole. Let us read this verse again with that definition in mind: The leper said, "Lord, if You CHOOSE, you can make me clean." Jesus replied, "I CHOOSE to make you clean." The faith that both Jesus and the leper released was based on choosing; it was released through their will. It was an act of choosing that activated faith and made the leper clean.

The will of man is the connector for the spirit and the soul. It is the place where decisions affecting our spirit, soul, and body are filtered. Without your will, you cannot make decisions concerning anything since it is the center of choice. For you to make correct choices, your will must be renewed through the power of God's Word.

Emotions

The voice of emotions is the voice of feelings. Although God created our emotions, the voice of emotions was never intended to be the ruling voice within our lives. Emotions must be subjugated to the will and spirit of man. If the voice of emotions is given the helm of your ship, it will lead you astray.

Emotions will naturally respond to the environment; they react to the feelings and actions of others. It is the part of you that is sensitive to **how** things are said more than **what** was said. It is the feelings center of your human makeup.

It can easily be argued that emotions have the loudest voice within you. While the spirit of man is the still small voice, the emotions are the loudest and most impressive voice you experience. Regardless of what the feeling may be, the emotions shout. Unfortunately, the voice of emotions can hinder correct hearing and decisions. They can cloud the arena of your life with smoke that makes it difficult to see and navigate clearly.

Generally, never make decisions based on emotional feelings. The voice of emotion can trick and deceive you into making a decision that is flawed. It will produce knee-jerk reactions rather than calculated responses. When emotions are running high and shouting at you, it is not the time to make a choice or decision. I can almost guarantee that in those situations, the choice will be incorrect and will lead you down a wrong path.

The Strong Voice

The voice of emotions is extraordinarily strong. It can influence your will to such a degree that improper decisions are made. It can shout so loud at times that other voices become inaudible. For this reason, decisions should never be made when the voice of emotions is the prevailing voice. We must discipline ourselves to discern the voices we are hearing and refuse to be moved by our feelings.

In the lives of Christians, the voice of emotions will often disguise itself as the voice of the Lord. Let me give you an example. Someone has their feelings hurt at their local church because of something said by another person. They are distraught and in emotional pain because of the occurrence. They pray about what they should do. Unfortunately, because their emotions are freshly wounded, they can only hear the voice of emotional hurt and pain. But, because they are praying and seeking the Lord, the voice they hear is believed to be the voice of the Holy Spirit.

They hear a voice declare that separation from those people who harmed them is the right course of action. The voice of emotions tells them it is time for them to find another church body where the people will really love them. They end up being deceived by the voice of their own emotions. The devil is nowhere around to trick them; it is the voice of their raw emotions that is shouting so loud that they can hear nothing else.

"For if anyone thinks himself to be something,
when he is nothing, he deceives himself"
(Galatians 6:3).

47

Paul said that it is possible to deceive yourself. Satan and demons do not have to be involved for one to be deceived. Deception happens when we believe the wrong thing. Believing that the voice of emotion is the voice of the Lord will cause us to be deceived by our own self.

I have seen believers deceived by the voice of emotions. It usually happens when someone becomes offended. The emotional response to the offense becomes deafening within their lives. They can hear nothing other than someone wronged them; they are angry, retribution is in order, and separation is right. Unfortunately, I have seen many good people led astray because they could not discern the voice they were hearing.

It is difficult to hear clearly when the voice of emotions is shouting. It can be overwhelming at times. The only way to overcome these situations is to allow your spirit man to take the ascendancy. You must tune in to the voice of the spirit and hear through the clutter of the feelings and emotions.

Don't Act When Emotions Shout

Generally, you should never make any decision when emotions are shouting. Even if it is a good emotion, do not let that be the ruling voice in your decisions-making. The choices people make in an emotional moment are usually wrong. I've witnessed people making these kinds of decisions in numerous areas and arenas of life.

Let me give you an example. A Christian woman is physically attracted to a man. She then dates him and finds many things appealing about him. From there, she "falls in love" with him, becoming emotionally involved with him to the point where she discounts the fact that he is not a Christian. Even though she knows that she should not be involved romantically with an unbeliever, her emotions of fondness and attraction are so overwhelming that she fails to hear her spirit saying, "This is wrong."

From there she decides to marry him. After they are married, she finds out he has a chemical addiction. He successfully hid it before they were married, but now it is out in the open, and he refuses to change. He also will have nothing to do with church or the things of God. Ultimately, all these issues lead to disagreement, strife, and division in the home. Divorce begins to be discussed as a possibility. She stops herself and asks, "How did I get here?"

There is an answer to her question. It is that she allowed her emotions to be the ruling voice in the decisions she was making. From the moment that emotions got involved, it became difficult for her to hear anything else. Her feelings and emotions deceived her into thinking that everything would be alright. The voice of emotions convinced her that she could change the man and be his salvation. However, she was deceived by a voice only meant to react and respond, not make decisions.

I have witnessed so many believers fall into the trap of being emotionally driven. Their decisions were determined by how they feel rather than the voice of the Lord and conscience. It usually does not turn out well for them; many times, it is disastrous. All the pain believers experience from these kinds of bad decisions can be avoided if they refuse to be led by the voice of emotions.

Regardless of the area of life, when people allow emotions and feelings to be the deciding voice, there will be consequences. It can be decisions concerning new purchases, vacationing, eating, travel, houses, furnishings, etc. The voice of emotions is not supposed to be the primary determining factor for your life.

Why Do We Have Emotions?

So, why did God give us emotions and feelings? It is because we would be nothing more than robots without them. One of the things that make us humans is the ability to experience emotional feelings. It is the part of our human existence that allows us to feel pleasure, love, and excitement while also allowing the feelings of sorrow, loss, and pain.

Feelings are not necessarily bad or evil. However, we must understand that we should not be ruled by that voice because emotions and feelings can change like the wind. They are not a reliable voice from which you can make most decisions. None of us can afford to be controlled by the voice of emotions.

Since emotions and feelings fluctuate, those who are controlled by them will be unstable in their decisions and actions. They will live their lives based on the whim of the moment. If it feels good, they act on that momentary feeling.

God created us with emotions and feelings but did not intend on these voices leading and guiding us. We are to be led by the Spirit rather than the voice of emotions. The voice of feelings was never intended to be at the helm of your ship. They are along for the ride and experience as the Holy Spirit leads us.

One of the fruits of the spirit is temperance; it is also known as self-control. I have never met anyone that possessed that fruit while being led by the voice of emotions. The result of being led by your emotions and feelings is inconsistent and damaging behavior. Those who have problems with self-control are usually living by the voice of emotions.

Not all emotions and feelings are bad. While joy is a fruit of the spirit, it is also an emotion that we should experience. Peace is another fruit of the spirit yet is something designed for us to experience emotionally. There are many other good emotions; however, the voice of emotions is not to be the voice that leads and guides us down the path of life.

You are a spirit, you have a soul, and you live in a body. Everything we do should be in that order. Our spirit man is first. It serves as the spiritual existence and communication center of man. The soul should be subservient as it is the hub of human and natural existence. Lastly, the body responds in accordance with other voices as the hub of our physical existence.

We must ensure that we can distinguish and discern the voices and where they originate. Failure to do so will lead to confusion and poor decisions. Proper placement and perspective of these voices will cause believers to experience the peace of God and freedom of the Spirit.

VOICES

4

THE BODY—
HUB OF PHYSICAL EXISTENCE

> Or do you not know that your body is a temple
> of the Holy Spirit in you, whom you have of
> God? And you are not your own, for you are
> bought with a price. Therefore glorify God in
> your body and in your spirit, which are God's
> (1 Corinthians 6:19-20, MKJV).

The body of man is what we can refer to as our earth suit. It is not the real you. It is the part of you that gives you access and allows you to function on the earth. Without your body, you cannot function, nor can you live on this planet. Your natural body is your basic mode of transportation while living in a fallen world.

The apostle Paul said that if the body were dissolved, we would have a heavenly tabernacle. He was speaking primarily of the spirit of man since it is the tabernacle of the Holy Spirit. Your body gives you the ability to work and be productive. It allows us to witness, preach, pray, and prophesy. Your body enables you to live and function as a human being on planet Earth.

Your body is an essential part of your trichotomy. Without the body, you cannot fulfill your destiny, which is one reason why it is important for us to take care of it. Paul said that your body is the temple of the Holy Spirit. No spiritual ministry can take place without it. Your ministry within the local church cannot happen apart from your body being involved.

All three parts of your trichotomy have a voice. Your spirit man has a voice and is the hub of spiritual existence. Your soul (intellect, will, and emotions) has voices and is the hub of human existence. Your body has a voice and is the hub of physical existence on this earth.

So, as human beings, we are comprised of spirit, soul, and body. Each part of our being has a voice. They all have a defined purpose, and they all speak. It is essential to be able to distinguish each of these voices. Every believer will hear all of them at different times in their lives. Discerning what voice is speaking is paramount to making correct decisions.

Languages of the Body

The voice of the body is designed to inform us of things that we are experiencing physically. When you feel pain, it will scream. Why is this? The voice of the body is telling you about something that has the potential to harm you. For instance, if you touch a hot stove, you will feel pain that the voice of your body communicates. If your body fails to inform you through the communication of pain, you might unknowingly cause irreparable damage to your body. When you are fatigued, your body will speak to you that it is time to rest. When your body is hungry, it will say, "Feed me." These are some of the different languages of your body.

The voice of the body is placed there by God Almighty. He created and designed it when He made Adam and then Eve. Its purpose is to inform you of physical things that need to be addressed for the safety of your existence. If your body is hurting in an area, it is usually telling you that something needs attention. Our total well-being is dependent upon us acknowledging this voice with the corresponding action.

We must understand that our bodies are a good thing—a temple of the Holy Spirit, as we read earlier. Paul goes on in this passage of Scripture to say that we are bought with a price and are to glorify God with our bodies. If our bodies are His temple, then we should take care of them. If we belong to Him, then we should totally surrender our bodies to the Lord. He bought it; therefore, He owns it!

> I beseech you therefore, brothers, by the mercies of God to present your bodies a living sacrifice, holy, pleasing to God, which is your reasonable service (Romans 12:1, MKJV).

In this verse, it is interesting that Paul speaks of presenting our bodies to the Lord. This reveals that the body is to be subjugated to the spirit and soul of man since an intentional decision is required to offer it as a living sacrifice. The voice of the body is not to be calling the shots. The body is presented to the Lord as an act of submission and servitude.

The Prominence of the Body in Culture

The reality is that we live in a culture where the body is often exalted. We see this in media, television, and magazines regularly. The body of man is given a place of preeminence in our culture today. It is the part of your trichotomy that people will evaluate first because it is the first thing they encounter.

Before someone has an opportunity to fellowship with you, they will see your body. It will create a first impression.

The scientific community will define you as a living being that is a body first. They will even say that the mind, intellect, and emotions (the soul) are a product of the body. They will completely ignore the fact that you have a spirit since it cannot be seen or touched. However, in the kingdom of God, it is the exact reverse. You are a spirit, you have a soul, and you live in a body—quite a difference from the scientific community at large.

As Christians, it is important that we do not approach life from being a body that possesses a spirit and soul. Things will be out of order, and we will listen to the wrong voices if we do. It is imperative that we live our lives from the perspective that our bodies are not what first defines us.

We are a spirit, just like God is a spirit. God also has a soul and body. How do I know that? Well, besides there being numerous Scriptures that indicate this, we are made in the very image of God. That means we look like Him. That means He looks like us.

The primary purpose of the body is to be your "earth-suit." It is the clothing that our spirit and soul wear. It enables the real you to function in the earth. Without a body, you can do nothing. Your body gives you the authority to function and operate within the physical realm where we live.

> And the LORD God formed man of the dust
> of the ground, and breathed into his nostrils
> the breath of life; and man became a living soul
> (Genesis 2:7, KJV).

In this passage of Scripture, we observe the creation of Adam. Through it, we can specifically see all three aspects of man's trichotomy.

God first created a body for man, formed from the dust of the earth. God used the content of the ground to form a body for Adam to inhabit. He used the minerals, vitamins, and makeup of the planet to create an earth suit for man to live in while walking on the planet. A point to note, the vitamins and minerals that are in the ground are still the things we need for survival of the body.

Then God breathed the breath of life into the body He created. The word translated "life" is the Hebrew word *neshâmâh* and is also translated in other places as "spirit." We can see here that God made man a spirit being.

Proverbs 20:27, which we shared in an earlier chapter, says that "the spirit of man is the candle of the Lord." The word "spirit" in that verse of Scripture is also the Hebrew word *neshâmâh*. So, when God breathed into man *neshâmâh*, he was made a spirit being. He was not merely a physical body that inhaled oxygen and exhaled carbon dioxide. His existence equally became a spiritual one.

The writer of Hebrews refers to God as the "Father of spirits" (Hebrews 12:9). It is important to understand that God is the creator of spirit beings. He made the angels who are spirit beings, which are "ministering spirits" sent to minister to those who are heirs of salvation (Hebrews 1:14). All the creatures around the throne of God that we read about in the book of Revelation are spirit beings. So, man is a spirit being.

After God breathed the breath of life into Adam's body, he became a living soul. The physical brain God created that was housed in man's body came alive. Man's will, intellect, and emotions started functioning. Adam began his spiritual, intellectual, emotional, and physical existence on Earth. He was a living and breathing human being.

Once again, we see in Genesis how God created man, spirit, soul, and body. He created man's body from the dust. He breathed a spirit into man. Then man's soul came to life. Man is not merely a body with a mind. Man is all three: spirit, soul, and body.

At the time of creation, Adam was given the ability to communicate with God. He enjoyed times of communion with the Father in the cool of the evenings; this was a time of dialogue, discussion, and instruction. God communicated His heart to Adam along with directives that he was to carry out. Among these were to maintain the garden, name the animals, and avoid eating certain things. God communicated with Adam everything he needed to know to navigate his existence on Earth successfully. There was no sin, fear, or shame. There was perfect harmony as every voice that Adam was designed to know and hear was unhindered in their ability to communicate properly.

Once Adam and Eve sinned, everything changed. God's perfect creation began a cataclysmic shift. A perfect garden of beauty became prone to thorns and thistles. A perfect human body was now subject to sickness, disease, and infirmity. Communion with God was dismissed from man's daily agenda as communication was shut down. The place of sinless perfection became broken and tarnished with the effects of iniquity. That which was birthed through God's love turned into a breeding ground for hatred and murder. All of this happened because of sin, and sin happened because someone listened to the wrong voice. Think about it!

The Big Zonk

Do not think for one moment that listening to illegitimate voices will produce anything but disaster. The voices to which you give power in your life matter. Listening and heeding the wrong voice at the wrong time can have catastrophic effects. It certainly did with Adam and Eve, and we are no different.

Adam and Eve gave place to the voice of the serpent. They were deceived into believing that eating the forbidden fruit would cause them to be wise and more like God. However, it caused the exact opposite. They sold their home, health, and family for a bite of a piece of fruit. Talk about a bad deal; that was a horrible transaction. It is as if they were on the television show "Let's Make A Deal" and got the biggest "Zonk" of all time. This all happened because they listened to an illegitimate voice. We will talk more about this in a future chapter.

Thank God, in the fullness of time, Jesus was sent to redeem mankind. He was the perfect lamb of God to take away the sin of all man. He suffered, bled, and died for the remission of our sins and then was raised from the dead for our justification. In His propitiatory act, Jesus paid the price to put man back in the place from where Adam fell. Communication with the Lord was restored as the Holy Spirit came to make His dwelling place in our mortal bodies. Hallelujah!

Our bodies have now become carriers of the glory of God. It is now the throne from where the kingdom of God exerts its power and dominion. The heart of man, housed in the body of man, is where the kingdom of God now dwells. Jesus said that the kingdom of God is within you:

> And when he was demanded of the Pharisees, when the kingdom of God should come, he answered them and said, The kingdom of God cometh not with observation: Neither shall they say, Lo here! or, lo there! for, behold, the kingdom of God is within you (Luke 17:20-21, KJV).

Notice what Jesus said when he answered the Pharisees. He said that the kingdom does not come with observation. In other words, the kingdom of God cannot be seen in the natural realm. No one can point to something or someplace and say that it is the kingdom of God. Jesus said the kingdom of God is within you. It is housed in your body. The kingdom of God is received when you become a new creation in Christ Jesus. It is then that your body becomes the temple of the Holy Spirit. The rule and dominion of God's Kingdom is not a geographical location because it is within the heart of every Christian.

Jesus came to make that a living reality. The primary goal of receiving Jesus as Lord is not merely to escape hell and go to heaven. Rather, it is to be the living demonstration of the kingdom of God manifested on the earth through the daily lives of believers in every realm of society. We are to live our lives inside out; the goal is to get the kingdom that is on the inside to be manifested on the outside. We are to be living demonstrations of His Kingdom.

Now, the only way this can happen is to possess a body that will allow it to take place. This is the reason your body is so important. Your body is to be the physical expression of the kingdom of God within the earth. Everything you say and do should be a direct reflection of God's Kingdom rule and reign on the earth.

The plan of God is for us to reflect the fullness of His glory in the physical realm where we operate, which requires our bodies to be submitted to the correct voices. We cannot reflect His image in the earth while listening to the wrong voices.

Here are some good questions to ask yourself: Am I a reflection of the glory of God through my physical actions? Do I look like Jesus, or do I look like the world around me? What am I reflecting through the words I speak and the actions I do?

> Therefore, when He came into the world, He said: "Sacrifice and offering you did not desire, but a body You have prepared for Me" (Hebrews 10:5).

Jesus needed a body to accomplish the will of the Father. A body was required for Him to minister the Word, heal the sick, cleanse the lepers, and raise the dead. He needed a body to fulfill His redemptive role as the sacrificial Lamb of God. Redemption could not have been realized without the physical body of Jesus.

Our justification was consummated the moment His body was resurrected. It was Jesus' body that bore the scars that signified He paid the price for the sin of all mankind. The body of Jesus gave Him authority to operate within the earth and made an opportunity for His ministry to be fulfilled. Everything Jesus did required the existence of a physical body.

Likewise, God needs our bodies to accomplish His plan and purpose on the earth. Just as Jesus needed a body to accomplish the will of the Father, your body is a necessary component for that to be achieved. Our bodies play an important role in the achievement of God's purpose within the earth. We use our bodies in every aspect of ministry function here on the earth, and without a physical body, there is no spiritual ministry.

Listen to Your Body

We must listen to the voice of our body when it legitimately speaks to us. When it says "rest," we should rest. When it says, "I'm out of shape," we should do something about it. Ignoring the voice of our body is not faith; it is failure to acknowledge a legitimate voice that is present to protect you. Faith doesn't negate the physical realities of the body; it merely believes God's promise when faced with adverse contradictions.

Several years ago, I began to experience some discomfort in the middle of my chest. At first, I thought it was just indigestion. So, I attempted to self-medicate. Unfortunately, it did not alleviate the symptoms but only increased with every passing hour. I finally told my wife, Stacey, "I think I need to go to the doctor," and we set up an appointment.

I explained the symptoms I was experiencing to the doctor, and he took his stethoscope out to listen to my heart. Upon examination, he immediately said, "I hear a rub." He proceeded to say, "This sounds like a pericardial rub akin to pericarditis." Well, I had never heard of such a thing. So, he performed an EKG in his office.

He came in with the results of the EKG. He said, "It looks like you're having a heart attack, and you need to get to the hospital." Upon hearing this, I went vagal. I turned white, and my wife thought something severe was happening (like being told you are having a heart attack is not). I kept telling her that I was fine. Truthfully, I was fighting with a spirit of fear at that moment.

The hospital was only ten minutes away, so we jumped in the car and took off. When I got to the hospital, they performed a routine examination and numerous tests. All tests came back normal, but they confirmed that I had pericarditis, a medical term for inflammation of the pericardial sac where the heart is seated. There is no specific cause as it is usually a secondary infection. Every time my heart would beat, it would rub against the pericardial sac resulting in chest pain. They admitted me into the hospital, treated it with some anti-inflammatory medicines, and kept me in the hospital for several days.

What I did not realize at the time is that if this had remained untreated, I could have died. Responding to the voice of my body by seeking medical help kept me alive. I was never in a life-threatening situation, but failure to seek help could have led to that place. This is my example showing why it is essential to take care of your body and listen to its voice.

The voice of the body is usually neither good nor bad; it is amoral. Its one function is to inform you of the condition of your earth-suit—the inescapable vehicle that enables you to traverse the road of life that must be maintained. If you don't heed the warning lights, you will break down.

All automobiles have warning systems. These systems are connected to gauges, lights, onboard computers, and even cell phone apps. If there is an issue with the automobile we are driving, it will notify us that something needs attention. Failure to act has the possibility of leaving you stranded alongside the road. Likewise, when our bodies notify and inform us of something that needs attention, we should heed the information. If the warning lights are illuminated, then do something to fix it.

I'm convinced there are many Christians who die prematurely solely because they discounted the voice of their body. They ignored the alarms and flashing lights. They failed to give attention to something that needed to be repaired and maintained. Ultimately, their earth-suit broke down on the highway of life. Let this not be our story.

Learn to respond appropriately when your body speaks. You need your body to accomplish God's purpose for your life. Be thankful for the body that God gave you and be a good steward of it.

5

THE FLESH—
HUB OF SINFUL EXISTENCE

> For those who live according to the flesh set
> their minds on the things of the flesh, but those
> who live according to the Spirit, the things of
> the Spirit. For to be carnally minded is death,
> but to be spiritually minded is life and peace
> (Romans 8:5-6).

Another voice that is important to recognize is the voice of the
flesh. Many people confuse the flesh with the body. When we
see the word "flesh" used by the apostle Paul, he is not referring
to the physical body. Rather, he is referring to the carnal
unrenewed mind and its appetites.

The flesh is given its voice through the unrenewed mind.
When our minds are renewed, it shuts down the voice of the
flesh. It is silenced and robbed of its ability to speak because
our minds are renewed to the Word of God. Thus, the
importance of renewing the mind cannot be overstated if we
desire to see victory over the flesh.

Many Christians confuse the flesh with the body. As we
discussed in the previous chapter, the body is amoral; it will do
whatever your mind instructs it to do. In general, the body will

only object when it feels sick, weary, hungry, or sleepy. Otherwise, the body does not argue with the will or intellect. It does not argue with your spirit either. The body is the vehicle that you inhabit for your physical existence.

The flesh is a totally different aspect of your being. The flesh is not an entity like your spirit, soul, or body. The flesh is the result of the work of sin that seeks to capitalize on certain desires which have some of their origins in the desires of the body and carnal thinking. However, the voice of the flesh is not the voice of the body. It is important to understand this.

Many believers confuse the flesh with the "old nature." I've heard people say that they have difficulty with their old nature. They fail to realize that the old nature no longer exists when someone is born-again.

"Therefore if any man be in Christ, he is a new creature: old things are passed away; behold, all things are become new" (2 Corinthians 5:17, KJV).

It's important to recognize that once someone is saved, the old nature no longer exists within their life. The old man is dead; he is crucified with Christ. The new man is alive on the inside of you. Your spirit that was separated from God is made alive. You are a new creation, and the old man is dead!

Failure to recognize that the old man (nature) is dead results in believers fighting the wrong thing. The problem is not the old nature; it is the voice of the flesh. It is unbiblical beliefs coupled with habits and behaviors that have been developed. Fleshly life patterns evolve because of ungodly behavior that one has practiced and seen exampled.

The voice of the flesh will always lead to sinful behavior. The flesh is unruly and full of wickedness. The flesh capitalizes on unbridled desires that seek to be fulfilled. It is at the root of all sinful and ungodly behavior.

Let's look at how the voice of the flesh is empowered to work.

> Let no one say when he is tempted, "I am tempted by God"; for God cannot be tempted by evil, nor does He Himself tempt anyone. But each one is tempted when he is drawn away by his own desires and enticed. Then, when desire has conceived, it gives birth to sin; and sin, when it is full-grown, brings forth death (James 1:13-15).

Notice that fleshly temptation begins when a person is drawn away by their own lust. It does not say that they are drawn away by the devil. Lust is the language of the flesh. Both *Strong's Exhaustive Dictionary* and *Thayer's Greek-English Lexicon of the New Testament* define "lust" as a longing and desire for what is forbidden. It is the desire for what is unholy and impure. So, where does this originate? It starts in the unrenewed mind that couples with natural carnal desires of the body. Most all ungodly lust involves gratification of some aspect of your personage through a biblically forbidden means.

As an example, the lust for sexual gratification seeks fulfillment outside of God-ordained parameters. It will seek illicit relationships outside of marriage. It will seek satisfaction through an unauthorized means. Lust seeks gratification through an illegitimate channel that God has forbidden.

God created sex to be enjoyed by a husband and wife within the boundaries of marriage. The marriage bed is to be kept undefiled. There is a proper manner for natural sexual desire to be fulfilled within human beings. However, fleshly lust seeks to find satisfaction through unsanctioned means that God forbids.

The language of lust, which is the voice of the flesh, seeks self-gratification. It cares nothing about anyone else; it is totally self-seeking. Therefore, just by this alone, it is sinful.

Conversely, love is not self-gratifying. Love seeks the welfare of others while the flesh seeks its own pleasure. The voice of the flesh will exalt and promote self. The voice of love will seek the benefit of others.

At the beginning of creation, temptation and lust were present. This means that the voice of the flesh existed in Adam and Eve. Read this account in Genesis:

> So when the woman saw that the tree was good for food, that it was pleasant to the eyes, and a tree desirable to make one wise, she took of its fruit and ate. She also gave to her husband with her, and he ate (Genesis 3:6).

In this verse, we see the temptation in which Eve indulged involved an appeal to natural carnal appetites. She saw it was good for food, pleasant to the eyes, and desirable for wisdom. She was drawn away of her own lust by the seed of desire and appetite. Eve elevated the natural desires above God's command.

We see the origins of sinful behavior revealed in this account—the lust of the flesh, the lust of the eye, and the pride of life. Carnal lust will always shout justifications for its behavior, while the conscience of man says the behavior is wrong. Most people who fall prey to sin will heed the voice that is shouting the loudest, the voice of the flesh.

The entire process with Adam and Eve probably went something like this. Eve saw that the fruit was good for food. After all, there is nothing wrong with a good meal. God placed the tree in the garden anyway. Why would He not want you to enjoy it? You are hungry right now, so indulge yourself! Eve saw that it was pleasant to her eyes. That fruit looked so delicious. It was the best looking fruit in the entire garden; it was beautiful to behold. So, it will definitely be good to eat.

Eve believed it would make her wise, and she would be like God. After all, what's wrong with being like God? Shouldn't we all receive wisdom and be like Him? She probably believed she would be a better assistant to Adam if she would just eat of the tree.

You can see all the justifications that the voice of the flesh will make for sinful behavior. Most all fleshly behavior is connected to some type of legitimate appetite. However, when the voice of the flesh violates God's command, we must allow the voice of the Holy Spirit to take the driver's seat. If we fail to do so, we will make the wrong choice.

Starve It to Death

One of the things that we can do to help diminish the voice of the flesh is starve it. If you don't feed it, it will die. The voice of the flesh is fed when you read or look at things that are fleshly in nature. The more you feed the flesh, the louder its voice will be in your life. Refraining from reading and watching things that are carnal will cause that voice to be minimized in your life. It will be too weak to utter a word.

Paul commanded Christians to crucify their flesh. He said that we should kill the flesh. That means the flesh is something we must contend with and that we should be merciless to it.

In an actual crucifixion, a person dies of asphyxiation. They are robbed of their oxygen because of the nature of this horrific death. We must deny the flesh of its oxygen. We must remove the source from where it is empowered. That means we avoid anything that empowers that voice within our lives.

What Voice Will Lead?

In the following passage of Scripture, I have intentionally added things in parentheses to bring emphasis and application.

> I find then a law: when I will [voice of the will] to do the right, evil [voice of the flesh] is present with me. For I delight in the Law of God according to the inward man [voice of the spirit]; but I see another law in my members [voice of the flesh], warring against the law of my mind [voice of conscience], and bringing me into captivity to the law of sin being in my members [voice of the flesh]. O wretched man that I am! Who shall deliver me from the body

> of this death? I thank God through Jesus
> Christ our Lord! So then with the mind [voice
> of the renewed mind] I myself serve the Law
> of God, but with the flesh [voice of the flesh]
> the law of sin (Romans 7:21-25, MKJV,
> emphasis added).

I shared this passage of Scripture to point out how different voices war with each other. Paul said there was an internal war going on inside of him. Various voices were competing for a position of leadership in his life.

It is imperative to understand that the only way to make the right choice is to listen to the right voice. Right choices are always the byproduct of listening to the right voices. Wrong choices are the byproduct of listening to the wrong voices. When anyone listens to the wrong voice and promotes it to the leadership position in their life, improper decisions will be made.

Paul asks the question of how he can see victory amid this war with the flesh. He then gives the answer: The key is to hear the voice of conscience and the renewed mind. Paul said that with the (renewed) mind, he serves the law of God. He recognized that he must listen to the still small voice and renew his mind to God's commands and promises to overcome his flesh.

We must feed our spirit and renew our minds to overcome the voice of the flesh. It is through Jesus, the voice of the Lord, that we experience victory. We must tune what we think and believe to what God has said and is saying.

Fleshly Justification Enables Sinful Behavior

We must understand that the flesh will always attempt to justify its behavior. Fleshly justification is one of the primary things that empowers the flesh to produce its sinful fruit. The voice that excuses ungodly conduct and fleshly indulgence is one of the most common things that the enemy will use to get believers off course. When a person believes something wrong and sinful is actually right and holy, there is nothing to keep them from doing it.

I've seen believers engage in fleshly behavior while believing they were doing the right thing the entire time. They justify their behavior with arguments and excuses that the carnal mind will communicate. Ungodly behavior is licensed in their lives because they give heed to the voice of the flesh.

King Saul justified his disobedience with the language of the flesh. He was commanded to wholly destroy the Amalekites and all their livestock. However, he brought back the best of the livestock and spared the life of King Agag. When confronted by the prophet Samuel, Saul made excuses and justified his disobedience. He said that the people influenced him, and he only did it to enable sacrifices to be made to the Lord. However, Samuel told him that obedience was better than offering a sacrifice.

The bottom line is that Saul justified and excused his sin. This is how the voice of the flesh operates and functions. It will excuse and justify that which God calls sin and disobedience. We must discern this voice and disallow it in our lives. This will be discussed in detail in my next book, *Voices of Deception.*

Going back to something that was said earlier, the voice of the Lord will never speak anything contrary to the written Word of God. Those who justify sinful behavior in the name of "the Lord told me" commit the same error of King Saul. They use a spiritual justification for immoral conduct. The truth is that they are mistaking the voice of the flesh for the voice of the Lord.

The Voice of the Flesh is Deceptive

I have seen people do all sorts of ungodly things because they believed God spoke to them. I have witnessed people lie, cheat, steal, divorce, commit adultery, stir up strife, and many other fleshly behaviors because they believed they heard the Lord speak. They mistook the voice of the flesh for the voice of the Lord, thereby justifying their sin with a spiritual excuse. Discernment is key to avoid this grave error.

The voice of the flesh is deceptive in nature. Eve was deceived at the beginning of time through fleshly justifications. She sinned because the forbidden thing was appetizing to the flesh. When she listened to the wrong voice, it brought sin into humanity. All the sins of the world can be attributed to an individual listening to the wrong voice. Think about it!

The voices you listen to and heed have a profound effect. It impacts your future and others. It is not merely a simple decision where you have the right to choose. Understand that the right to make a choice does not make your choice right. It is imperative that we make the right decisions by listening to the right voices.

The voice of the flesh will always seek to be promoted. It will appeal to the basest human desires. It will attempt to gratify through illegitimate means. Just say, "No!" Allow your spirit man to rise and muzzle the voice of the flesh with the Word of God.

6

THE HOLY SPIRIT— VOICE OF CONFIRMATION

"But when the Helper comes, whom I shall send to you from the Father, the Spirit of truth who proceeds from the Father, He will testify of Me... However, when He, the Spirit of truth, has come, He will guide you into all truth; for He will not speak on His own authority, but whatever He hears He will speak; and He will tell you things to come. He will glorify Me, for He will take of what is Mine and declare it to you" (John 15:26, 16:13-14).

In the following three chapters, I will discuss the voice of the Holy Spirit. There are three specific attributes and manifestations on which we will focus: the voices of confirmation, confrontation, and conviction.

The Holy Spirit is the spirit of truth. Anything the Holy Spirit speaks will be true. This means that the voice of the Holy Spirit will always be in agreement with the written Word of God. This is one of the most important principles we should establish in talking about the Holy Spirit.

Discerning the voice of God begins with a knowledge of the Word of God. Believers must have a good understanding of the Bible to properly distinguish the voice of the Holy Spirit. Those who do not know the Word will easily be led astray by voices that come to deceive. Paul said that even satan comes as an angel of light and illumination. So, even someone who has a heart after God can be fooled if they do not have a good foundation of God's Word in their life.

The Holy Spirit Confirms the Word

The Holy Spirit's voice will confirm what is already written in the Bible. He will not speak things that are contrary or contradict. Since He is the same yesterday, today, and forever, what He said in days past, which has now been canonized, is still true today. It has not changed.

So, one of the primary functions of the voice of the Holy Spirit is confirmation. He speaks to confirm what Jesus already said. "Confirm" means to support further, strengthen, and re-establish. The voice of the Holy Spirit will not tear down, change, or weaken what God has already spoken and made plain. Any voice that does those things is not from God; it is the voice of the enemy.

Jesus said that the Holy Spirit would testify of Him. The voice of the Holy Spirit is in total agreement with the words of Jesus. He will speak and testify of the same things that Jesus spoke while walking the face of this earth. His purpose is to confirm what has already been spoken. Anything that is contrary to this can be discerned quickly as the voice of a stranger.

The Voice of the Stranger

It is amazing to me how many believers will still follow the voice of the stranger. Most of the time, it is because they do not know the Bible. The enemy will deceive them because of their ignorance of God's Word. The enemy will disguise his voice to sound like the voice of God. Those who are not intimately familiar with God's voice can easily be led astray in this situation. Having intimate knowledge of the written Word enables believers to rightly discern His spoken Word.

As a pastor, I've had people come into my office and say that God spoke to them. When they shared with me what they believed God said, I knew immediately that they had listened to the voice of a stranger. I knew this because it was contradictory to biblical principle that was already clearly established. Yet, their lack of knowledge became the doorway whereby they were convinced of something that was false.

> "My people are destroyed for lack of knowledge. Because you have rejected knowledge, I also will reject you from being priest for Me; Because you have forgotten the law of your God, I also will forget your children" (Hosea 4:6).

Notice that God attributes the cause of destruction to the lack of knowledge. He did not say it was the devil or demons; He said that ignorance is what caused people to be destroyed.

Ignorance can be produced in two primary ways. The first way is through neglect. This is where someone, by choice, fails to acquire knowledge. The second way is rejection which happens when someone refuses to hear the truth because they do not like it. It does not fit with what they want to believe or a certain narrative to which they have ascribed, so they reject knowledge. Whether someone fails to acquire knowledge through neglect or refuses the truth through rejection, it will still produce destruction in their life.

Biblical Ignorance Is Dangerous

We must understand that ignorance is not bliss in the kingdom of God. Operating in ignorance is inexcusable for believers today. Knowledge abounds everywhere. The real issue is that believers are distracted because of television, social media, the internet, pleasure, etc. Many have given greater value and time to things that distract rather than the Word of God. Therefore, biblical illiteracy has become the rule of the day.

This illiteracy has contributed to the deception that can be seen manifesting in the Church. When there is a lack of understanding and knowledge, opinions and truth have nothing against which to be measured. This results in the evaluation of validity being based solely on emotional feelings and natural intellect, which leads to great error. Therefore, there must be a biblical standard established for proper assessment of anything said to be from the Lord. The Bible is the first and primary standard for this to be done.

The Holy Spirit's voice will always confirm what Jesus said. He does not confirm our opinions. He does not confirm any incorrect doctrine. Instead, He confirms the words of Jesus. Why is this? It is because Jesus said the Holy Spirit would testify of Him. With that in mind, let's look at this verse of Scripture in Revelation:

"...I am your fellow servant, and of your
brethren who have the testimony of Jesus.
Worship God! For the testimony of Jesus is the
spirit of prophecy" (Revelation 19:10).

The Holy Spirit will testify of Jesus; He utters the testimony of
Jesus. He does not speak of Himself; He speaks of Jesus. The
Spirit says what Jesus says. Therefore, all prophecy will be what
Jesus is saying. This means that all legitimate prophetic
utterances will be in perfect agreement with the words of Jesus
that are written in the Bible. Likewise, it means that prophetic
directives will be in accord with the conduct and behavior that
Jesus demonstrated and promoted.

If you want to know what Jesus is saying today, then read what
is recorded that He said yesterday because it has not changed.
Therefore, that which the Holy Spirit speaks will be in
harmony with the words of Jesus that are recorded in the Bible.

One of the purposes of the gift of prophecy in the Church is
confirmation. While prophecy is not limited to confirmation,
many times, the prophetic words that are spoken confirm
things that we may already spiritually sense the Lord is
speaking to us personally. Again, the spirit of prophecy is the
testimony of Jesus.

Always the Same, Never Changing

The Holy Spirit will not contradict Himself. His voice is not
schizophrenic in nature. He does not say something and then
change His mind. The voice of the Holy Spirit is consistent. If
we hear things that continually change, we can rest assured that
the Holy Spirit is not involved. He is not confused, nor does

He vacillate. He is constant and never changing in His will and purpose for our lives. There may be new things that He reveals that we have not yet known, but He is not continually changing every day.

The Holy Spirit has been sent to lead and guide us; Jesus said that He would guide us into all truth. The Greek word that is translated as "guide" means to show the way. The voice of the Holy Spirit is designated to show us the way that we should go. He reveals to us where we are to turn, go, and stop. He shows us the path of life and leads us away from the path of destruction. This is His function within the lives of believers.

The Holy Spirit will reveal to you the future. He is within us to unfold God's purpose for our lives. To do this, He speaks to us. It is impossible for any of us to arrive at a correct destination if we do not know where and what it is. The voice of the Holy Spirit will speak to us about the destination God has planned for us. He will talk about what God has in store for us after we arrive. He will prepare us for potential dangers that may be present on the road He has designated for us to travel. The Holy Spirit reveals these things so that we will arrive alive.

Arrive Alive

Interesting enough, for many years, there was a highway motto that was promoted in the state of Florida, "Arrive Alive." This campaign emphasized obeying the speed limit along with driver safety. It is important to realize that a primary purpose of the voice of the Holy Spirit is to enable us to "arrive alive." God desires that we fulfill our purpose and destiny in Him and gives us the Holy Spirit to be our GPS on the road of life. He will provide us with turn-by-turn directions to help us safely arrive if we listen to and heed His voice.

Our future is a total mystery until the Holy Spirit speaks and reveals portions of it to us. He will do that if we are willing to listen to His voice. As Jesus said, the Holy Spirit will speak to us of things to come. He speaks to us about what God has planned for our future, which enables us to prepare and believe for what is in God's heart to be fulfilled within our lives.

I can recall throughout my life how the Holy Spirit has revealed things to me concerning my life and ministry. He has always been faithful to reveal the things that were to come. This gave me hope and expectation for what He was preparing for me to receive, experience, and accomplish.

A Change of Direction

At the beginning of 1996, I began to hear the Holy Spirit speak to me in my prayer times that He was preparing me to plant and pastor a church. At the time, my wife and I, with our three children, were living in our hometown of Panama City, Florida. We were conducting itinerate ministry events both nationally and internationally. Things were going very well and smoothly. In the natural, there was no reason to change our course. However, God had a change of direction, and He was speaking this change to me through the voice of the Holy Spirit.

In June of that year, we were on our way to Indianapolis, Indiana, to participate and minister in a Christian International Conference. As we were traveling, I began to converse with my wife. I told her that I felt the Holy Spirit had been speaking to me about starting a church. She was shocked and surprised. She immediately began to ask questions of how, where, when, and who and declared that she would not have a church in our house. I answered her by saying that I had no idea and only God knows.

After completing the conference in Indianapolis, we were scheduled to minister on the following Sunday in an inner-city local church. Upon completing my ministry in the service, the pastor asked if they could minister to us prophetically. She immediately began to prophesy about a church that we were going to start and that it would be in the area that we lived in presently. Wow!

Neither my wife nor I had spoken to anyone about starting a church. However, the Holy Spirit was confirming within both of us that He was leading us down this road. They went on to prophesy that a dance studio would be our portion. Interestingly enough, we started our church in a dance studio.

I shared that story to show you how the voice of the Holy Spirit will reveal and then confirm. While His voice is revelatory, it is equally confirming. After receiving those prophecies, we knew that God was speaking and leading us to plant and pastor a local church. We were confident that God was actively involved in this commission that He had given us.

The Holy Spirit Will Glorify Jesus

Jesus said that the Holy Spirit would glorify Him. Another way we could say this is that the Holy Spirit will bring glory to the Lord, not a man. The purpose of the voice of the Holy Spirit is not to glorify or praise a man; it is to glorify and exalt the name of Jesus, His work in the earth, His Kingdom, and His Church.

The word "glorify" means to honor and magnify. When you magnify something, you make it larger. The voice of the Holy Spirit will make the work of Jesus larger in our lives. He does not come to magnify our egos, status, or appearance in the eyes of others; He comes to make Jesus greater than every other name, person, or entity. This is what the Holy Spirit will speak.

There are many people today who are expecting the Holy Spirit to glorify them. They desire to hear a word that will exalt them personally in the eyes of others. However, the voice of the Holy Spirit has not been given to stroke our ego or raise other's opinions about us. Instead, His voice will glorify and exalt Jesus. Remember, the testimony of Jesus is the spirit of prophecy which is the voice of the Holy Spirit articulated. The Holy Spirit will always exalt Jesus.

The Holy Spirit Will Breathe Life

It is important for us to recognize that the voice of the Holy Spirit is life-giving. His voice brings life to those who will hear Him. He does not come to condemn; He comes to breathe life. His voice is intended to resurrect that which should be alive and thriving. His voice is life-giving and will bring things together.

Let's look at how the voice of the Holy Spirit brings life and resurrection:

> Again He said to me, "Prophesy to these bones, and say to them, 'O dry bones, hear the word of the LORD! Thus says the Lord GOD to these bones: "Surely I will cause breath to enter into you, and you shall live. I will put

sinews on you and bring flesh upon you, cover you with skin and put breath in you; and you shall live. Then you shall know that I am the LORD.'"" So, I prophesied as I was commanded; and as I prophesied, there was a noise, and suddenly a rattling; and the bones came together, bone to bone. Indeed, as I looked, the sinews and the flesh came upon them, and the skin covered them over; but there was no breath in them. Also He said to me, "Prophesy to the breath, prophesy, son of man, and say to the breath, 'Thus says the Lord GOD: "Come from the four winds, O breath, and breathe on these slain, that they may live."'" So I prophesied as He commanded me, and breath came into them, and they lived, and stood upon their feet, an exceedingly great army (Ezekiel 37:4-10).

The Holy Spirit took Ezekiel to an open graveyard. We call this the Valley of Dry Bones. God instructed Ezekiel to prophesy to the dead bones that were scattered there.

As Ezekiel began to release the voice of the Holy Spirit, the bones came together. Then sinew, muscle, and flesh came on the bones. There was a total reconstruction of human bodies that took place. Then the Lord said for him to prophesy and release breath to go into the corpses. He obeyed, prophesied, and it happened. The result was a resurrection of living, breathing human bodies. They were representative of what God would do in the nation of Israel.

If you notice in this account, nothing happened until Ezekiel prophesied. Nothing took place until the voice of the Holy Spirit was released into the situation. Life was empowered, and death was abated the moment that His voice was released. Understand that prophecy is the voice of the Holy Spirit being articulated through an individual. It is the expression of the heart of God through a human vessel under the unction of the Holy Spirit.

This demonstrates one of the reasons that the Holy Spirit must have an outlet to release His voice. He looks for a man or woman that will allow Him to speak through them so that life can be brought forth amid devastation. The Holy Spirit needs a man or woman who will yield their voice to clearly articulate what God is saying. He cannot do it by Himself; He must have a willing vessel who yields to His voice. One of the major hallmarks of the voice of the Holy Spirit is that it will breathe life into dead situations.

The Voice of Jesus in the Earth

Recall that Jesus said the Holy Spirit would testify of Him, He would not speak of his own, and He would glorify the Lord. If Jesus came to bring life, then the voice of the Holy Spirit will be life-giving. The Holy Spirit is a continual reflection of everything that Jesus came to accomplish and do within the hearts of men. This means that the voice of the Holy Spirit is the voice of Jesus in the earth. There is no disagreement or contradiction. Jesus came to bring us life, and so it is the same with the Holy Spirit.

It is imperative that we understand these concepts and truths if we are going to properly discern His voice. Failure to comprehend these things causes believers with good intentions to err in their way. It causes those desiring to speak accurately to say ill-advised things in the name of "the Holy Spirit told me."

The Voice of Salvation and Restoration

The voice of the Holy Spirit does not come to condemn people; it is satan who does that. Jesus said that He did not come into the world to condemn it but that the world would be saved (John 3:17). He did not come to beat people over the head, remind them of all their evil deeds, and sentence them to torment for eternity. Jesus came to save them.

Since Jesus came to save, then the voice of the Holy Spirit is sent to say and do the same thing. His voice does not condemn. Paul said there is no condemnation to those who are in Christ Jesus. The Holy Spirit will convict us, yet He does not condemn us. This is true because Jesus does not condemn, and therefore, the Holy Spirit will not do it either. We will talk more about this later in this writing.

The heart of God is always to restore. Jesus said that He came to seek and to save that which was lost. He came to restore what the devil had stolen through the fall of man. When Adam and Eve sinned, they lost everything; they literally lost their home, the Garden of Eden. They lost their relationship with God. There were no longer any evening strolls with the Lord or communion with Him. The nature of man became perverted, and sin assumed a preeminent position within their lives. This ultimately led to the first murder when Cain killed his brother Abel.

Jesus came to restore and regain what man lost. He came to restore the relationship. He came to erase the heart of hate and replace it with a heart of love. He came to fill the emptiness within the heart of man that sin had produced; Jesus came to fill the longing and void. He came to restore everything that man forfeited through sin.

With this in mind, we understand that the voice of the Holy Spirit comes to bring restoration. He does not come to rob or steal; He comes to fill us with that which is missing. The Holy Spirit is not looking to exclude anyone. Rather, He is looking to receive all who will believe and receive.

In the story of Job, God gave him double what he had lost. This is the heart of God in manifestation:

> You have heard of the perseverance of Job and seen the end intended by the Lord—that the Lord is very compassionate and merciful (James 5:11b).

The end that God intended for Job was a double portion of everything that he lost. We see that the nature of God is to restore. He will truly give you double for your trouble! He is willing to turn things around in our lives so that the end is better than the beginning. This demonstrates the very nature of God.

God's Nature and Voice Are Inseparable

We cannot separate the nature of God from the voice of the Holy Spirit. The moment we justify a separation, we cannot say that it is His voice speaking. The Holy Spirit will always speak in perfect harmony and agreement with the nature and heart of God. Anything different violates biblical precepts and principles. Just as God's nature is to restore, so is the voice of the Holy Spirit.

Jesus' ministry was redemptive. He came to redeem mankind from the hold of the devil. He came to purchase us from the prison that sin had created. Since Jesus' ministry was redemptive, so is the voice of the Holy Spirit. His voice will be laced with redemption and restoration. The Holy Spirit will testify of Jesus and His character. His nature is to redeem and restore man to the place from where he fell.

The reason that the apostle Paul said that prophecy edifies, exhorts, and comforts is because that is within God's nature (1 Corinthians 14:3). He desires to build us up, exhort us to move forward, and comfort us with hope that lies ahead. His character is love. Therefore, what the Holy Spirit speaks will manifest His nature of love. He cares for His people, so His voice will express that care and compassion.

The voice of the Holy Spirit is not purposed to tear us down; rather, He builds us up. His voice is not to discourage, rather encourage and exhort. He speaks to give us hope and expectation, not depress us with a fatalistic outlook. He desires to strengthen, not weaken.

We can never separate God's character from His voice. In hearing the voice of the Holy Spirit, we must always factor the nature of God. This is an important principle that helps us properly discern His voice. If what we are hearing disagrees with the nature of God, then we are responsible to dismiss it and acknowledge that it is not a legitimate voice to be heeded.

Knowing His Voice by Understanding His Nature

We know His voice by understanding the nature of God. We can quickly disregard voices when we know they are contrary to His character. People who know me also know my character. They know how I act and behave. Their observance of my character has formed their knowledge of who I am. Likewise, we know His voice because we can recognize His nature in what we hear.

When believers embrace illegitimate voices, it always leads to destruction. Many are deceived because they improperly discern. They wrongly perceive because they do not know how to properly evaluate and judge what they are hearing. The truth is that when you improperly perceive, you will be deceived.

Paul said there are many voices. We must understand that there is no shortage of voices in the earth. However, most of them are illegitimate and should not be followed. The first way we can properly discern is through a knowledge of God's Word, which includes a proper understanding of His character and nature. An improper understanding of God's nature will cause believers to miss it. This, in turn, will cause them to walk down the wrong road that will ultimately produce negative consequences.

The voice of the Holy Spirit comes to confirm. He will confirm the words of Jesus. He will testify of Jesus. He will speak in agreement with the character and nature of God. His voice will build us up and make us strong. Knowledge of these truths will help us hear His voice clearly. We will be those who follow the voice of His Spirit, and a stranger we will not follow (John 10:4-5).

VOICES

7

THE VOICE OF CONFRONTATION

> And it came to pass, when Joshua was by Jericho, that he lifted his eyes and looked, and behold, a Man stood opposite him with His sword drawn in His hand. And Joshua went to Him and said to Him, "Are You for us or for our adversaries?" So He said, "No, but as Commander of the army of the LORD I have now come." And Joshua fell on his face to the earth and worshiped, and said to Him, "What does my Lord say to His servant?" Then the Commander of the LORD's army said to Joshua, "Take your sandal off your foot, for the place where you stand is holy." And Joshua did so (Joshua 5:13-15).

The Holy Spirit's voice will confirm within us what Jesus said, what He has done, and what He is doing in our lives. His voice will echo what is being said and heralded in heaven. The Holy Spirit operates within the realm of this earth. He is the agent sent to communicate God's plan and desire for man.

Since we live in a fallen world, there are fallen ideas and beliefs that must be confronted. We need to address these actions and deeds that are harmful to the life of a believer. For change and proper conformity to take place, these things must be confronted. The voice of the Holy Spirit is here to do that and help us eradicate the things that are not in agreement with God's plan for our lives.

The God Who's in Your Face

In the previous passage of Scripture, it declares that the Lord "stood opposite" Joshua. Another way we could say this is that the Lord was in Joshua's face. The Lord confronted him before He was to fight the first battle in Canaan.

As you read the account, Joshua asked the Lord a question concerning whose side He was on. Joshua was concerned about who was on his side as the leader of the Israelites. The Lord responded with the word "No." I believe the Lord was saying that the question was not to be whose side He was on, rather who was on His side as the commander of the army of the Lord. The Lord confronted an inaccurate perspective and perception that Joshua held.

Here we see a picture of the way God works in the lives of believers. God expects us to conform to Him. Those who are asking God to conform to their way of thinking and believing are requesting the wrong thing. They are asking the wrong question. It is not about God taking our side; it's about us taking His side. It is not about God agreeing with us; instead, it's about us agreeing with Him and His Word.

The Holy Spirit will confront things within our lives that are not in agreement with God's Word, will, and way. His voice will confront areas of our lives that are not aligned properly with His plan for man. Just as a Father confronts a child, so will He confront the areas where we need adjustment.

Confrontation before Inheritance

It's important to note that Joshua was confronted BEFORE he went into Canaan, the Promised Land. We must understand that God confronts before He conveys inheritance. The reason the Lord does this is that we will lose and forfeit our blessing if actions, thinking, and believing are not first augmented. He will confront those things through the voice of the Holy Spirit so that He can lead us into our land of promise.

Confrontation does not come to hurt you, rather to take you to the next level of fulfilled destiny and purpose. Before Joshua could begin taking the territory that he was commissioned to possess, he had to be confronted by the Lord. There had to be adjustments made, and then he was given a battle strategy that would bring about victory and triumph.

While the Holy Spirit will confront us in our own personal prayer and study, He will also use ministry gifts within the body of Christ to be His agents of communication. He will use apostles, prophets, pastors, evangelists, and teachers to speak into our lives to prepare us for what lay ahead. The Holy Spirit will use anointed men and women to confront things that would otherwise keep us from moving forward in divine purpose and destiny.

It is important to understand that this aspect of confrontation may be accomplished through the voice of the Holy Spirit speaking directly to us, or through another vessel of His choosing, or through both. Regardless, it is still His voice confronting issues within our lives that need to be corrected.

Confrontation for Correction

In 1988, I was a staff member of Christian International Ministries. I had been working there for about a year when I began to feel some discontentment. One day in prayer, I felt that I heard the Holy Spirit tell me that it was time for me to resign. I then shared that with another individual that was a part of the ministry. Much to my surprise, they turned around and shared this with the head of the ministry, Bishop Bill Hamon.

I received a call from Bishop Hamon, and he requested a meeting with me. I went to his office, where we began to discuss things. He brought up what he had been told about me considering resigning my position at the ministry. I admitted to him that I had said it. I also told him that I felt that the Holy Spirit had spoken this to me.

Then, much to my surprise, he said to me, "The Holy Spirit is not telling you to leave; the Lord actually wants you to make a five-year commitment." Wow, I was taken back. He went on to say that he believed that God would bless and further my ministry if I would make that commitment and get settled. I agreed to do so.

I had just experienced a confrontation from the Holy Spirit, who was speaking through an anointed vessel to deliver a word of correction and adjustment in my life. My perspective was skewed and needed to be aligned. God providentially positioned things so that He could redirect me by the voice of the Holy Spirit operating through someone's life and ministry.

The reality is I was hearing the voice of discontentment speaking to me while it disguised itself as the voice of the Lord. I was being deceived by the voice of feelings and emotions. It was not the voice of the devil, rather the voice of inner frustration and ambition.

Many times, what has been referred to as deception from the enemy is merely self-deception. Improperly discerning and distinguishing the voices we hear will cause us to deceive ourselves. It will cause us to be thoroughly convinced that God spoke something to us when He did not say anything. This is a trap to which believers succumb and are led astray. Listening to the wrong voice has caused many good people to err. We are not to be led by the voice of discontentment and ambition; we are to be led by the voice of the Holy Spirit.

Listening Produces Blessing

Thankfully, I had someone in my life who was willing to speak the truth. All of us need someone that we will allow to speak truth to us. Typically, this would be your pastor or another reliable fivefold ministry gift. It can also be your spouse or family member who can properly discern the voice of the Holy Spirit. We should allow them to speak into our lives and give great weight to their counsel because it will keep us from dangers that we would otherwise encounter on the road of life.

After I agreed to a five-year commitment., things began to break through in our lives. Within six months, Stacey and I were able to purchase our first home. Songs that I had written were being recorded by Integrity Music, and I was asked to lead worship on their worship CD, *Victor's Crown*. Financial blessings began to overtake us.

There is always a blessing on the other side of obedience. Listening to the right voices will produce the manifestation of God's favor and promotion within your life. The favor of God that is released through obedience will open doors and opportunities that our abilities and hard work could never accomplish. Hearing and heeding legitimate voices will be the key to unlocking heaven's best for our lives.

Confrontation Prepares Us

When the Lord confronted Joshua, He did so to bring an impartation. Joshua needed to be properly equipped to be empowered to accomplish and fulfill the plan of God. For forty years, he had been faithful to Moses; he was second in command and had served the man of God throughout their wilderness journey. When a new day arrived, He needed a new anointing.

Throughout their forty-year journey, Joshua had only been involved in two battles. They were fed by manna from heaven daily. There was a cloud by day and a fire by night to lead and guide them. Then, in one day, it all ceased.

Now they would have to depend on the prophet and priest for guidance because there would be no more external guideposts. The Israelites would need to get their own food by robbing the beehives and milking the cows in the land that flowed with milk and honey. Now they were required to fight regularly to take a land that was possessed by giants, walled cities, and armies much larger than theirs. It was a new day.

In Your Face So You Can See

Before Joshua could take possession of Canaan, the Lord introduced him to an aspect of His character that was unfamiliar. The Lord revealed that He was a warrior. When He appeared to Joshua, He had his sword drawn. His intention was not to use it against Joshua, rather to reveal that He was the Lord of Hosts, the captain of the armies of heaven.

There was no way for Joshua to be a warrior without knowing that his God was one first. We all emulate what we see. In the moment of this confrontation, Joshua needed to see the Lord in a dimension that was previously unknown to him. It required the warrior nature of the Lord to be demonstrated and manifested before his eyes. God got in Joshua's face to reveal something that he needed to see.

God confronts us with the voice of the Holy Spirit so that we will see things we have not previously seen. He confronts us to reveal things about His nature and our need to conform. The purpose of confrontation is change, not personal destruction. It comes to elevate us to a position and place higher than we were previously.

We must be confronted to conform to the image of Jesus. It does not happen automatically, and it does not occur solely because we love the Lord. It happens as truth confronts the issues within our lives that are not in alignment with God's Word, precepts, and principles. Change and conformity happen on the other side of confrontation. The Holy Spirit has been sent to do that within our lives.

We must understand that God is not interested in making us feel good; He is interested in making us godly. He is not attempting to appease our flesh, rather see it crucified. The role of the voice of the Holy Spirit is not to produce some sort of feeling or sensation of ecstasy; instead, the goal is to cultivate holy and righteous living that glorifies the name of Jesus.

The Voice of Love

The voice of the Holy Spirit is the voice of love. Since God is love, His voice will articulate and communicate the same. He will not speak something to us from a disposition of hatred or condemnation. Love is the motivation of everything that He speaks. This is the way and manner in which He will communicate to His people.

An important principle of love is to understand that it will confront. Love does not enable wrong decisions or behavior. Love will not sit idly by while someone unknowingly self-destructs. Love will confront the issues head-on and seek a remedy to deal with root causes.

Disabling and destroying roots in our lives that would later bring destruction is a role of the voice of love. Ungodly roots and attitudes will produce undesirable results and cause the foundation of our lives to be uneven and eventually crack. These roots must be removed before God can build properly within us and through us.

Root Removal

My wife and I built a house in 2016. Some trees and bushes were removed because they were in the way of the footprint for the house. There was a magnolia tree, a couple of pine trees, an oak tree, a couple of small shrubs, and numerous palmetto bushes, and all this vegetation had roots. The trees could not be merely sawed off at the ground and the bushes mowed; the roots of all these things had to be totally removed. If we attempted to build on top of the roots and stumps, major issues in the foundation would arise later. To build the house properly, we had to remove the undesirable roots.

As believers, if we want our spiritual house to stand, we must remove the undesirable roots. Root attitudes, beliefs, and actions that do not agree with God's Word must be eradicated. Since we have lived with many of these things for years, we need help seeing them clearly. The Holy Spirit is here to reveal these things and then enable us to eradicate them.

God will speak to us personally to bring deliverance and freedom. He will also use people in our lives to assist with the process. God is faithful to speak to us if we will listen. He loves us so much that He will not allow us to remain the way we are. The Holy Spirit will speak and confront the issues that seek to destroy us because He is the voice of love.

A Biblical Pattern

Throughout the Bible, God raised up prophets to confront things His people were doing that were incorrect or sinful. We can read where prophets confronted kings and leaders because of immoral behavior, primarily in the Old Testament. Since the Holy Spirit did not inhabit individuals during that time, His voice could only be heard through the prophet and priest or someone He anointed at a specific moment. The Holy Spirit was incapable of dwelling within people because there was no way for man to be born-again. Yet, we can observe within Old Testament accounts how the Holy Spirit would deal with His people and confront things that were sinful.

Moses confronted Pharaoh and said, "Thus says the Lord: 'Let my people go'" (Exodus 8:1). God spoke through Moses to a wicked ruler to let the Israelites go free. Pharaoh rejected the Word of the Lord, and the plagues of Egypt ensued. Eventually, Pharaoh relented and granted the Israelites the freedom that God demanded. However, when Pharaoh decided to go back on his promise of freedom to the Israelites, he and his army were drowned in the Red Sea.

Rejecting confrontation from the voice of the Holy Spirit can produce negative consequences in the lives of believers in the same way that was seen in the life of Pharaoh. If we refuse to heed the warnings and dealings of the Lord, we set ourselves on a collision course with disaster. We must take heed to His voice so that we will avoid these types of things and live in the blessings of God.

Elijah confronted Ahab and Jezebel by speaking out against their idolatry and Baal worship. He called for repentance throughout the nation. This resulted in a showdown at Mount Carmel between Elijah and the prophets of Baal. After God consumed the sacrifice with fire from heaven, Elijah instructed that the prophets of Baal be destroyed. Once again, those who fail to respond correctly to the confrontation of the Holy Spirit will reap destruction.

Jesus confronted the Pharisees. John the Baptist confronted Herod. Nathan confronted David. Samuel confronted Saul. God even used a donkey to confront a false prophet.

There are numerous other places throughout the Word of God where we see the confrontation of the Holy Spirit in the lives of people. It is an important ongoing function of His voice within the body of Christ. We must receive it and respond correctly.

Confrontation Is Not Condemnation

Unfortunately, many believers have perceived confrontation as condemnation, but it is vital to know the difference. **Confrontation** will shine the light on areas of your life that need to change while offering hope, restoration, and redemption. **Condemnation**, on the other hand, will accuse and sentence someone with no opportunity for redemption or restoration. It is a sealed fate—a declaration with no hope.

As we discussed previously, everything the Holy Spirit speaks is redemptive and restorative in nature. He is not seeking to drive people away from Him, rather draw them near to Him. The Holy Spirit will gently move people to take steps toward the Lord, not away from Him. He desires to save, heal, and deliver.

For a surgeon to remove tumors or growths that could possibly cause someone to die, he must confront it. Ignoring it will not save the individual. The doctor is required to remove the life-threatening anomalies through surgical procedures that may involve an incision, clamps, stitches, staples, etc. There will probably be some pain associated with it before, during, or after the removal. It is all a part of the process of eradicating something that could rob someone of their life.

Spiritual Surgery

Many times, there are things growing in our lives that are not godly. Those things require the voice of confrontation to come and surgically remove them so that we can live in the kingdom of God as fruitful believers. The Lord is the Great Physician; He will faithfully remove and eradicate the spiritual abnormality within our lives with His two-edged sword, the written Word, and the voice of the Holy Spirit. This will cause us to live and thrive in the kingdom of God.

Anyone rejecting the work of a surgeon to remove something dangerous could result in their death. Likewise, refusing the voice of confrontation can result in separation from God's best for our lives. Just like the surgeon is attempting to save the life of his patient, the Holy Spirit is seeking to bring salvation, healing, and deliverance to the ones He confronts. His love for us compels Him to deal with the things that seek to destroy us.

Correct responses to the voice of the Holy Spirit will result in the blessing of the Lord being released within our lives. Rejection of confrontation will be reaped in consequences and pain. As the prophet Samuel told King Saul, "Obedience is better than sacrifice." We must hear **and obey** the voice of the Holy Spirit and allow Him to work in our lives.

8

THE VOICE OF CONVICTION

And when He has come, He will convict the
world of sin, and of righteousness, and of
judgment of sin, because they do not believe in
Me; of righteousness, because I go to My
Father and you see Me no more; of judgment,
because the ruler of this world is judged (John
16:8-11).

I know that most all Christians have heard of the conviction of
the Holy Spirit. Most believers reference it in relation to the
pricking of the heart of man that draws them to a place of
repentance. It is something we have traditionally associated
with the moment of salvation. An unsaved individual hears the
Word preached; they sense a conviction in their heart for the
need for salvation and then respond accordingly. However, the
voice of conviction is much more than that alone.

The word "conviction" literally means to convince. So, the voice
of the Holy Spirit comes to convince us of truth, the truth
concerning sin, righteousness, and judgment. The voice of
conviction is there to bring revelation and a knowing of things
that can only be revealed by Him. He convinces and persuades
us of the truth concerning our relationship with God.

Conviction to Bring Change

Conviction is the work of the Holy Spirit that convinces someone of the need for repentance and change. He convicts us of change that needs to take place within our lives. The first experience of an individual with the voice of the Holy Spirit is the conviction of sin. He speaks to us of the need to repent and make Jesus Lord of our lives. He convinces us that we are traveling down the wrong road and need to experience a change of direction.

This conviction is not to condemn or sentence a person; it is intended to draw someone to a place of decision and change. The voice of the Holy Spirit, manifested through conviction of sin, is designed to produce a heart-change within the life of a sinner. Man alone cannot convince someone that they need a spiritual change. The Holy Spirit is the only one who can do that. His role in the life of an unbeliever is to convict them of sin.

Once the Holy Spirit convicts an unsaved person, the correct response is repentance; there is a change of mind and heart. It produces a turning in their life to serve the Lord. Repentance is a change of mind, change of direction, and change in action. It also involves a sense of remorse for things that were wrongly done in the past, which is called godly sorrow.

Paul said that godly sorrow works repentance (2 Corinthians 7:10). There is a divine sense of sorrow when the Holy Spirit convicts one of sin, not to be confused with condemnation and guilt. Godly sorrow causes us to run to Jesus, not run away from Him. This remorse is intended to produce acts of repentance in response to the voice of conviction.

Blind Spots

There have been countless times in my ministry where I have counseled people. Many of these times, there was a need for change within the life of the individual. I told them of the necessary change, but they could not see or understand that it was needed. Those people had a blind spot, and I was unable to convince them.

A blind spot is an area of our lives that we cannot perceive. While others can see it, we are blind to the area. In these situations, we must depend on wise counsel and pray that the Holy Spirit reveals it to us. The reality is that people will not change until the issue is revealed, and they can see it. The voice of the Holy Spirit will illuminate it if we are willing to receive. We must open our hearts to the voice of the Lord so He can reveal to us the things that seek to destroy us.

The voice of conviction comes to show us these areas of our lives that we could not previously see. The Spirit speaks to reveal the areas that need to be adjusted. Change is the goal of the voice of conviction.

In the middle of a counseling session, I have heard people say, "I just can't see it." Unfortunately, their failure to recognize and see the issue is what empowered it to remain. Long-standing situations that were right under their nose could not be perceived because they had existed to the point of becoming part of their identity. They struggled to separate their behavior from who they were as an individual. Therefore, in their minds, to acknowledge the issue was to say that they were defective. The voice of conviction comes to bring that separation and reveal the difference. The Holy Spirit possesses the ability to enlighten the problem without condemning the person. He will shine His light so that we can see clearly and receive deliverance from that which has plagued us. He is faithful!

It is important to understand that man cannot convict the heart; this is a work reserved for the Holy Spirit. Only He can bring conviction of sin in areas where we missed the mark. Since the definition of sin is to miss the mark, the Holy Spirit will convict both non-Christians and Christians where they missed it. It is a work that He alone can do.

The Work of the Holy Spirit

Jesus said the Holy Spirit would convict the world of sin because they did not believe. The first role of the voice of conviction is to convince people to believe in Jesus. The Holy Spirit draws people to the Lord. A spiritual drawing to God is required for someone to turn to the Lord. Without it, a heart cannot be changed.

This aspect of conviction is to continue throughout the lives of believers. In the areas where we have not properly believed, the voice of the Holy Spirit will bring revelation about how to believe correctly. He will change our hearts so that faith can arise, and we will receive the promises of God. Thus, the voice of conviction is an ongoing work of the Holy Spirit within the lives of believers.

Conviction is the work of the Holy Spirit that convinces man about the need to repent and change. Regardless of how much you communicate with someone regarding their need to walk in a different direction, nothing will happen unless the voice of the Holy Spirit enlightens them to their deficiency. Only through the voice of the Holy Spirit can the heart of man realize the reality of the need for repentance.

Jesus said the Holy Spirit would convict of sin, righteousness, and judgment. Each of these three areas has a unique purpose in a person's life. It is the conviction of sin that causes someone to repent and receive Jesus as Savior. The conviction of righteousness reveals we are righteous and pricks our heart if we miss the mark. Conviction of judgment cultivates the reverential fear of God and produces boldness in believers as agents of the Jesus' authority to execute His judgment on demonic principalities.

The conviction of sin convinces man that he is sinful and needs a Savior. The conviction of righteousness convinces us of who we are in Christ and how we should live and behave. The conviction of judgment convinces us that God is just—One who will render justice. He will cause good to come on those who serve Him and recompense on those who reject Him and His commandments.

The Conviction of Sin

The conviction of sin is the aspect of the Holy Spirit's ministry whereby man is drawn to Jesus. All of us have experienced this prior to salvation. It is the voice of the Holy Spirit that speaks to our hearts and causes the realization that our sin has separated us from God to be birthed. It convicts us that the only solution to our dilemma is believing upon Jesus and exhibiting faith in His propitiatory sacrifice. When coupled with a confession of His Lordship, that conviction causes the fruit of salvation to be realized within our lives. We are born-again because of our correct response to the convicting voice of the Spirit of God.

In this passage from John quoted at the beginning of this chapter, Jesus said the Holy Spirit convicts of sin "because they do not believe in Me." Technically, it is not breaking the commandments that cause people to be separated from God; it is the sin of not believing upon Jesus. The greatest of all sins is the rejection of Jesus' sacrifice and is the sin of which the Holy Spirit first convicts. The solution for this sin is for man to believe in Jesus and receive Him as Savior. This is the first and primary work of the Holy Spirit. This is where it all begins, the conviction of sin.

The Conviction of Righteousness

The voice of the Holy Spirit continues in the life of the believer after salvation. He comes to convict of righteousness. This aspect of conviction causes a firm confidence to reside within a believer's life that they are right with God. It is like they never did anything wrong or committed any sin. That firm conviction is based on what Jesus accomplished through His death, burial, and resurrection.

It is the blood of Jesus that causes our sin to be blotted out. However, His resurrection enables us to be made the righteousness of God in Christ Jesus. We are now alive unto God and have been raised to the newness of life because we are born-again.

> Therefore, if anyone is in Christ, he is a new
> creation; old things have passed away; behold,

all things have become new... For He made
Him who knew no sin to be sin for us, that we
might become the righteousness of God in
Him (2 Corinthians 5:17, 21).

These verses of Scripture reveal the truths that the voice of the
Holy Spirit will reinforce in the lives of believers. He convicts
and convinces us that we stand holy before God and can
approach His throne boldly. He lets us know that we are
children of God and in a right relationship with the Father.
His voice fights against the spirit of condemnation.

His Voice Does Not Condemn—It Empowers

One of the greatest enemies to a believer is condemnation. The
reason for this is because it is impossible to fulfill purpose and
destiny if we are riddled with guilt and shame. It robs us of our
faith and confidence. It robs us of our right standing with God
and causes us to shrink back from doing what He has told us
to do. It releases fear and causes faith to subside.

The voice that condemns is not the voice of the Holy Spirit;
His voice is not the voice of condemnation. His voice is the
voice of the conviction of righteousness. While the Holy Spirit
produces a conviction and pricking within the heart of believers
if they engage in sinful behavior, He will not condemn or
pronounce judgment on any of us.

One of the reasons that the Holy Spirit does not condemn
us is because it robs us of the boldness necessary to
accomplish the purpose of God. **Since the Holy Spirit is
the one who comes to empower us to do the will of God,
He will never do anything to contradict or impede its**

fulfillment. Condemnation and negative judgment are things that prevent God's will from being performed in a believer's life. Therefore, the Holy Spirit does not speak the language of condemnation; He speaks the language of affirmation.

The Holy Spirit's voice will affirm and confirm who we are in Christ Jesus. He will speak to us about things we need to know concerning our destiny in God. His voice will empower us to do God's will and purpose. He will speak things that enable us to accomplish the things we are commissioned to do.

The Path of Righteousness

The conviction of righteousness is not limited only to who we are in Christ; it also involves knowing what is right and wrong. The voice of the Holy Spirit will confirm to us biblically righteous ways to conduct our lives while revealing the ways that are unholy. The Psalmist declares that He leads us in paths of righteousness (Psalm 23:3), which means His voice will never lead anyone down the road of sin.

The voice of the Holy Spirit will ALWAYS lead believers down the road to right and holy living. He will never tell us to do things that are sinful. Any voice that promotes immoral behavior is not the voice of the Holy Spirit. He will never excuse you to step outside the path of righteous behavior. The conviction of righteousness will convince believers of the necessity to constantly conduct their lives within the boundaries of biblical precepts and commands.

Many times, believers can begin to feel justified in doing things that constitute questionable behavior. They will make excuses for it while they ignore the conviction of righteousness. Mental and emotional arguments that are contrary to God's Word can begin to dominate one's life when they override the voice of conviction. If done enough, it can lead to having a seared conscience that gives a deaf ear to the Holy Spirit's voice of conviction. This is the danger zone!

We must be sensitive to the voice of conviction. If the voice of the Holy Spirit pricks our heart about anything, we should give heed, even if we do not like it at the moment. The flesh will want to rebel, but the spirit will say, "Yes!" Jesus said that the spirit is willing, but the flesh is weak. Your spirit willingly surrenders to the voice of conviction while the flesh desires to submit to sinful behavior. We must recognize the voice of conviction and discipline ourselves to obey it.

The Conviction of Judgment

Judgment is not a word that any of us like to talk about, but it is a biblical word and a good word when properly understood. Most people see biblical judgment as an angry God seeking to pour out His wrath. However, judgment is an act of love and mercy from the heart of the Father to preserve the man he loves from the consequences harvested through continued sin.

There are three different aspects of judgment that I will explain. These are applied truths of judgment in relation to what Jesus said:

> "And when He has come, He will convict the world of sin, and of righteousness, and of judgment... of judgment, **because the ruler of this world is judged**" (John 16:8, 11, emphasis added).

Jesus said that the conviction of judgment was because satan was judged. In this arena, the voice of conviction is directly related to what happened through the death, burial, and resurrection of Jesus. The Holy Spirit speaks of this judgment at the cross and then was ratified through Jesus' vicarious suffering and triumphant resurrection.

This aspect of the voice of the Holy Spirit confirms within us that we are victorious in Christ. It certifies that sin was judged at the cross, and we can now walk in victory with total freedom from its control and dominion. When we listen to this voice of conviction, we arise on the other side with boldness and authority.

Knowing that the sin of all mankind was judged at the cross, we get a different picture of judgment. We must see judgment through the lens of what happened when Jesus gave His life for our ransom. The judgment of all sin was laid upon Him. God's wrath was taken out upon Jesus as He was betrayed, beaten, scourged, nailed to a cross, and ultimately died, separated from the Father. Jesus literally became sin and received its judgment.

While a picture of mercy and grace to us, the cross is the greatest depiction of judgment that has ever been known to man. Jesus, as an innocent man, received the full judgment and penalty of ALL the sins of EVERY man. He took it all. He took my place; He took your place. He took all the judgment that belonged to us. As an innocent spotless lamb, He received the punishment and judgment of the vilest sinner.

In doing so, Jesus spoiled principalities and powers. He made an open show of them and then destroyed the one who had the power over death in His triumphant resurrection from the dead. The ruler of this world, satan, was judged through the substitutionary act carried out by Jesus. The one who had the power of sin was judged and declared powerless over those who would believe upon the name of the Lord.

Conviction of Our Authority

The voice of the Holy Spirit comes to convict and convince that the ruler of this world has been judged. This fact is now what gives us boldness to take authority within the earth. This revelation causes us to be fearless, knowing that the devil has no power in our lives. Understanding comes through the voice of conviction which gives us the ability to prevail in spiritual warfare.

The Psalmist said in Psalm 149 that we are here to execute the judgments of God upon the demonic principalities and powers. Without realizing that the devil has already been judged and lost his power, we will be unable to execute judgment effectively and prevail. The Holy Spirit desires for us to win, and He brings conviction that both the devil and sin's power have been judged already!

From this, we see three aspects of the conviction of judgment. The first being Jesus took our judgment. The second is that satan and sin were judged in Jesus' substitutionary acts. The third is that we have now been given the power to execute judgment upon the devil. The conviction of judgment is not that destruction awaits us, rather that we are victorious through Jesus! Hallelujah!

Eternal Judgment

There is one other aspect of judgment that would be irresponsible not to mention. We must understand that one of the foundational doctrines of the Church found in Hebrews 6 is eternal judgment. I believe that this doctrine encompasses the things that I previously mentioned but also includes the future judgment that is to come when we will all stand before the judgment seat of Christ. There, we will be rewarded for the things that we did in obedience to God's will and purpose for our lives.

It is the conviction of this judgment that produces a holy reverential fear of God within our lives. The fact is that there are consequences for sin and disobedience that we must never forget. When someone has no fear or consideration of the consequence of sin and disobedience, they become lawless and live a life of anarchy. This is dangerous.

While a person may be saved and dabble in sin at the same time, this is not God's best for anyone. The wage of sin is still death; the payday that disobedience brings is not pleasant. Continual sinful living will produce negative consequences within the lives of believers. Paul said that whatever a man sows, that is what he will reap. He went on to say that sowing to the flesh would cause one to reap the consequence of corruption. Another way of saying this is that the seed of sin sown will produce a resulting judgment. Judgment becomes the harvest of bad seed sown.

Living without consideration of the consequences of unholy living will cause believers to live without restraint or boundaries. Understanding that God said what He meant and meant what He said produces conviction. The voice of the Holy Spirit will convict us of the judgment that can take place in our lives now if we choose to ignore His leading. He will also convict and convince us that we are living for an eternal reward and not merely temporary satisfaction and momentary pleasure.

Yes, we have been redeemed through the blood of Jesus, and He took the judgment for our sin. However, if we continue to live in a lawless manner, we then forsake that afforded blessing and entangle ourselves again in the yoke of bondage. It is the balance of both understandings that causes us to live victorious in this life.

Pray that your spiritual ear will be tuned to the voice of conviction. It will help you along the path of life. It will cause you to live victoriously over the devil and his strategies. Hearing and heeding the voice of the Holy Spirit is paramount to us living as kings and priests in this life and showing forth His glory in the earth.

VOICES

9

THE VOICE OF PROPHECY

"But he who prophesies speaks edification
and exhortation and comfort to men"
(1 Corinthians 14:3).

The gift of prophecy is one of the nine manifestation gifts of the Holy Spirit spoken of by Paul. It is the only gift that we are specifically instructed to covet. This instruction indicates the importance of this gift to be in operation within the Church.

The voice of prophecy is the Lord speaking through His prophets and prophetic people. It is utterance and articulation that are inspired by the Holy Spirit. Prophecy is Jesus speaking through and to His bride, the Church.

All of us are familiar with the prophet's ministry in the Old Testament, where he would speak the word of the Lord as the Holy Spirit came upon Him. In the New Testament, we see both the ministry gift of the prophet and the gift of prophecy. Prophets will usually prophesy, but prophesying does not make one a prophet. All believers can function and flow in the simple gift of prophecy, but that does not make them a prophet.

It is the same voice of prophecy that operates in both the life of the prophet and the prophetic believer. God has ordained it within the Church to be a source of encouragement and hope. He has placed it within the body of Christ to encourage and strengthen believers. It is a gift that we should all participate in and embrace.

Jesus Placed Prophets in the Church

Jesus set prophets in the Church. When He ascended to the Father, with the release of the Holy Spirit, He sent ministry gifts. The prophet is one of those gifts within the five-fold ministry: apostle, prophet, evangelist, pastor, and teacher. These gifts are in the Church for the edifying and building up of the body of Christ. They are ministries designed to prepare and equip believers for the work of the ministry. They do not exist for the purpose of doing the ministry, rather enabling believers to do so.

Since Jesus set the gift of the prophet in the Church, it is needed; the Lord did not initiate anything within the body of Christ that we did not need. Prophets are crucial for the Church coming to a place of maturity and fullness of ministry to function in the earth.

One of the primary things that prophets will do is express the mind and heart of God through the voice of prophecy. They will speak the "now" word of the Lord. They will express the *rhema* of God to give direction and insight to the body of Christ. Thus, they will build up the Church and make it strong.

Prophecy Comes to Restore

It is important to always keep in mind that God delights in building people up, not tearing them down. Our God is the restorer, not the destroyer. The voice of prophecy in the Church aims to restore and reconcile people to their God-given purpose and destiny. It is to see families restored to the manner that God intended. The prophetic voice of the Lord comes to restore hope in those who are downtrodden, peace in those who are worried, love in those who are full of hatred, and purpose in those who have given up.

Many people believe that the voice of prophecy is intended for the pronouncement of judgment and punishment. Their mindset has been formed by the picture of an angry Old Testament prophet like Jonah. They understand the prophetic ministry to be a prophet arriving with a word of destruction for a territory or people. However, that is not the purpose of the voice of prophecy within the Church. God is not intending on destroying His people; rather, He desires to restore His people.

If God wanted to destroy people, He would not need a prophet to announce it to everyone. Even prophecies of judgment in the Old Testament possessed threads of redemption. If the people responded with a heart of repentance, the destruction would be abated. If they ignored the warning, devastation would ensue. In the story of Jonah, we see this prime example: Jonah prophesies to Nineveh, and the people repent, garnering God's mercy shown instead of destruction.

Old and New Testament Differences

Although God has not changed, some of the ways and means that He works and communicates with His people have been augmented in the New Covenant. For instance, in the Old Covenant, the Spirit of God did not dwell within the hearts of His people, nor were they born-again. To hear the voice of the Lord, one was required to approach the prophet.

In the New Testament, He dwells within those who believe, and His voice can be clearly heard by every believer. It is not necessary for New Testament believers to approach a prophet to hear the voice of the Lord. God can speak directly to us since He lives in us.

Much of the time, people will view prophecy through the lens of judgment. It is seen as the voice of the Lord articulating His displeasure and wrath upon humanity. Some view the ministry of the prophet and prophecy as vehicles by which God releases His anger and judgment within the earth because of man's sin. However, we must see prophecy through the lens of New Testament purpose and application.

Prophecy Is Redemptive

At Calvary, Jesus bore our judgment on the cross. He acquired the penalty for sin and unrighteousness, becoming sin so that we could be made the righteousness of God. Therefore, God now sees His people through the blood that Jesus shed. The greatest judgment that believers experience today is the harvest of bad seeds they have sowed. This is called the law of sowing and reaping in effect, not God actively releasing His judgment upon man.

Think about this: while you were yet a sinner, Christ died for you. We must see God through the light of redemption. We must see Him through the substitutionary work that Jesus accomplished at Calvary. Failure to do so will cause believers to misunderstand the purpose for the voice of prophecy within the Church.

Prophecy is the expression of the heart of God, which is redemptive in nature. The word of the Lord comes to call mankind unto Jesus, not reject them. He is not attempting to alienate the sinner from His mercy and restoration; rather, He is calling them to come close so He can make things better. His heart is not to punish humanity for their sin because Jesus bore that punishment already.

"...the testimony of Jesus is the spirit of prophecy."
(Revelation 19:10).

Since Jesus is the Word made flesh (the voice of the Lord within the earth), we must look at prophecy through the ministry of Jesus. His ministry was three-fold. It was redemptive, instructive, and demonstrative. Therefore, the voice of prophecy will speak the same things since it is the testimony of Jesus.

The prophetic voice of the Lord will be redemptive, articulating the principles that Jesus taught. It will also demonstrate the power and anointing of the Holy Spirit. If it is doing anything other than this, we must be cautious in our reception.

The testimony (voice) of Jesus is the spirit of prophecy, which means that the prophetic voice of the Lord will echo what Jesus said and is saying. It will never be contrary to the heart and

121

spirit of Jesus. If we cannot find Jesus doing it or saying it in the Word of God, then it is not an authentic voice of prophecy.

The Needed Voice in the Church

The truth is that God initiated the gift of prophecy within the Church because we need it. To think that we no longer need something that God ordained is the height of human arrogance. Man cannot survive and thrive in his own knowledge and understanding. Nor does man have all the answers to every situation that he encounters while living upon the earth. The voice of prophecy is within the Church to bring illumination and understanding so we can successfully navigate through the issues that we face in life and fulfill God's plan.

Saying that we do not need the prophetic ministry in operation is a statement of disdain for that which God says is needful. We must receive and embrace the gift of prophecy. However, we must understand God's divine purpose for this gift so that we approach it properly and use it correctly.

Purpose for the Prophetic Voice

We must understand God's purpose for everything that He initiates. God has given everything a purpose, a divine reason for its existence. If we fail to recognize that purpose, we will approach and use things incorrectly. It is imperative that we understand why God has placed the voice of prophecy within the Church.

The prophetic ministry is not a "crystal ball." It is not intended to merely shine the light on your future, while it may do that to some degree. Instead, the voice of the Lord is intended for the purpose of producing God's plan for our lives into full manifestation. It is designed to make us fruit-bearing believers.

> "For My thoughts are not your thoughts, Nor are your ways My ways," says the LORD. "For as the heavens are higher than the earth, So are My ways higher than your ways, And My thoughts than your thoughts. For as the rain comes down, and the snow from heaven, And do not return there, But water the earth, And make it bring forth and bud, That it may give seed to the sower And bread to the eater, So shall My word be that goes forth from My mouth; It shall not return to Me void, But it shall accomplish what I please, And it shall prosper in the thing for which I sent it. For you shall go out with joy, And be led out with peace; The mountains and the hills Shall break forth into singing before you, And all the trees of the field shall clap their hands. Instead of the thorn shall come up the cypress tree, And instead of the brier shall come up the myrtle tree; And it shall be to the LORD for a name, For an everlasting sign that shall not be cut off" (Isaiah 55:8-13).

This is a powerful and familiar passage of Scripture that reveals the purpose of the Lord's voice—the voice of prophecy. I can remember hearing these verses quoted regularly in my first exposure to the Word of Faith movement. It was specifically spoken in relation to the authority of God's Word in accomplishing His purpose and will. It was emphasized that the written Word of God would accomplish His will and prosper us.

In the context of this Scripture, Isaiah is speaking specifically of the Word that proceeds from God's mouth, His spoken word—His voice. This passage of Scripture is a declaration of the things that the voice of the Lord will accomplish and do within the earth. There are comparisons made that give us insight as to how the spoken voice of the Lord works and operates to bring things into full manifestation within our lives. This gives us an understanding of God's purpose for the prophetic voice of the Lord.

Reveal the Thoughts and Intentions of the Lord

The first thing that is specifically mentioned in this passage is that the thoughts and ways of man are not the thoughts and ways of the Lord. He speaks His Word and releases His voice to reveal and give understanding of His intentions and plans. Since man does not have the ability to fully comprehend these things with the natural mind, God releases His voice in the earth to give us insight.

Another familiar passage of Scripture verifies this concept. Jeremiah 29:11 declares that God knows the plans that He holds for us—plans to give us a hope and a future. This reveals that God has a good plan for our lives, and He desires to show it to us. He does not wish to keep it from us; He wants to communicate it to us. This is a critical understanding to have and maintain.

God is not attempting to hide His plan for our lives. While things may be momentarily undisclosed, it is not His plan that things remain in that manner. God wants us to know His plan and intention for our lives so that we can co-labor with Him. He does not desire for us to walk in the dark.

Failure to know God's plan and purpose will result in believers making wrong choices. It will cause mistakes along the road of life that can produce negative consequences and setbacks. It is imperative that we know His plan. Therefore, God releases His prophetic voice in the earth to allow man to know His desire and intent. He wants our desire to become conformed to His desire. He wants our ways to be conformed to His ways. He wants our thoughts to be conformed to His thoughts.

Navigating through Transition

Many years ago, my wife and I went through a season of transition. We did not know where we were going nor what we were to do. At the time, we were living with my parents with our two-year-old son, Joshua. It was not by choice or lack of diligence that we were in this situation; it was a divine repositioning happening of which we were unaware at that moment.

When we walk through transitional phases, we often fail to see the full scope of everything God is doing within our lives. Without prophetic insight, we are blind to what is transpiring.

It was during this time that we were invited to lead worship at a prophetic conference with Christian International. To be honest, coming from a Word of Faith church, we thought that the prophetic camp was a little strange and weird. However, God had brought us to the end of ourselves, and we were searching for direction.

At that moment and time, neither Stacey nor I knew where to go. We felt as though we were in spiritual limbo. Unknown to us at the time, God providentially brought us to a place where

His will and purpose for our lives could be revealed and unfolded.

The first encounter we had there was with a prophetess who declared that we were in the right place at the right time doing exactly what God wanted us to do. It is unbelievable how comforting that was to hear after beating myself up for months because of feeling like a failure for living with my parents. On a side note, we should recognize that a simple word of prophecy can make a profound impact on someone's life.

A week later, Bishop Bill Hamon prophesied to me, "I don't know if anyone has ever told you this, but there is a mighty prophet's call upon your life." I was 25 years old when he ministered that word to me. It confirmed what God spoke to me when I was 17 years old. I had only told one person, my former pastor, and he did not believe me; so, I never told another living soul. However, God knew it and quickly got my attention when it was spoken by Bishop Hamon.

These two prophetic words spoken to my wife and me caused the plan and purpose of God to begin to open before us. The plans that we had were tossed to the side, and we fully embraced what God was saying. The voice of prophecy caused our ways and thoughts to come into conformity with God's intent.

Direction Given through His Voice

When God reveals His purpose, it will give you direction. After those prophetic words were spoken, we knew God had called us to be part of a prophetic company. We began to make plans to submit to the leadership of Bishop Hamon and Christian

International. Just one month later, we were asked to join their staff. The rest is history.

You must understand that it was not my original plan to attend a Christian International meeting when I was asked to lead worship. I had no goal of becoming a staff member. However, when the voice of the Lord was released through the prophetic ministry, it caused my plans to change. My thoughts became His thoughts as His voice revealed things that I previously did not know. This is the power of the revealed purpose of God through the gift and voice of prophecy. It transforms our thinking and plans.

After these words were spoken over our lives, we had direction. If anyone is ignorant of knowing God's plan, they will continue to wonder and wander. God wants us to know His will. So, He placed the prophetic ministry within the Church to give voice to His plan for our lives.

It is so important that we understand that God is not hiding things from us. He does not want us to wander around with no direction for our lives. That is the lifestyle of a wilderness walker, not a Canaan conqueror. We are called to take our promised land and territory, not walk in the dark. Therefore, God speaks to enlighten us.

Water the Earth

The next thing we see in this Scripture passage is that the voice of the Lord will water the earth. It will refresh and revive the scorched land. It will cause life to return to the areas that have gone dormant. The prophetic voice of the Lord acts as rain that waters the dry places of your life.

Going back to the testimony of my first service at Christian International, Prophetess Jan Painter ministered to me, "You are one of God's today guys, and you've got to give out of what God is doing today." At that time, we were considering going back into a denominational church that did not embrace many of the present truths that we have now come to know and practice. The exhortation of the Spirit was that we could not go back; we must move forward.

It is amazing how simple prophetic words spoken through the anointing of the Holy Spirit will cause you to be revived and come alive. After receiving that prophetic word, we were given a recording of it. We had a one-hour drive home that night, and I distinctly remember repeatedly listening to that prophetic word all the way home. The more I listened to it, the more life I sensed being infused into me.

The truth was I needed watering; I was dry and thirsty and needing direction. It was the voice of the Lord that watered my dry, parched earth and caused me to come alive. I felt like I got my second wind and was ready to run again. This is the power that is released through the voice of prophecy when issued accurately, timely, and with the anointing of the Holy Spirit.

There are a lot of Christians who are spiritually dry, and they need to be refreshed and revived. I am not saying that they cannot hear the voice of the Holy Spirit for themselves in their own private devotional prayer and Bible study. However, there is a supernatural release of spiritual watering that happens when the prophetic voice of the Lord is released through an anointed vessel. This is something we all need at different times in our lives.

Understand this principle: **God's prophetic voice is designed to manifest in the middle of dry and lifeless conditions to produce rain and release life.** The voice of the Lord does not come to tickle our ears and stroke our ego. Instead, it comes to water and brings to life the things that are dormant and need to be resurrected. This is the power of the word of the Lord.

Make You Bud and Blossom

Isaiah went on to say that the voice of the Lord would cause the earth to bud and blossom. God's voice causes productivity. It will cause you to do things that you have never done or thought you would ever do. It will cause you to be fruitful in areas where you have not born fruit.

In February of 1988, my wife and I were ordained by Bishop Hamon. He declared this statement prophetically, "You will stand and prophesy by the hour." At that time, the most I had prophesied alone was about five minutes. I was new to some dimensions of the prophetic ministry and had only been on staff at Christian International for two months.

Ironically and providentially, I was scheduled to give my testimony a couple of days later at the Full Gospel Businessmen's chapter meeting in Panama City Beach, Florida. I went there thinking that it would be a short meeting where I would share my testimony which did not take a long time. I had no drug problems, alcohol addictions, or gang and imprisonment stories to tell them since I had been saved from the age of four and filled with the Holy Spirit since I was eleven. Mine was not the usual testimony that people came to hear at these types of meetings.

At the end of my short testimony, the president of this local FGB chapter announced to everyone present, "If there is anyone who desires to receive a prophecy, come and line up here on my left, and Brother Robert will prophesy to you." My heart sank the moment he said it. He had failed to inform me that I needed to be prepared to prophesy to anyone. He volunteered me on the spot. While I maintained a smile on the outside, there was an S.O.S. taking place on the inside; I was crying out to God for direction.

It was at this moment that the Lord reminded me of the word that I had received: "You will stand and prophesy by the hour." Then I heard the Lord say to me, "Follow the pattern." I then recalled everything that I had seen over the last several months of ministering with Bishop Hamon. I retraced the steps of what I saw him do when he prophesied to people.

By this time, people had lined up, and it seemed that the line stretched to eternity. It went down the side of the building and stretched across the back wall. In my book entitled *iBelong*, I speak in detail of all the steps I went through to follow the pattern. As I emulated Bishop Hamon, I stood and prophesied to everyone in the line, and it took almost two hours to minister to everyone.

I share this so you can see how the prophetic voice of the Lord released something within my life that had never been manifested. The voice of the Lord caused me to bud and blossom in an arena of ministry that had previously not existed. His word watered my earth and caused me to bear fruit.

Seed for Planting

Isaiah continued by saying that the Word of the Lord, the voice of prophecy, would provide seed for the sower. It is important to realize that what God speaks to us is a seed given for a future harvest that He desires to bring forth within our lives. His voice utters the seed we need to plant. So, God equips us to see success by giving us the seed that we need.

A prophetic word released concerning family restoration is a seed that can be planted to produce that harvest. It will result in prodigals returning to the fold and marriages being restored. God is not merely speaking to let us know of things to come in our future; His voice is being declared to give us a seed that we can plant to give us the desired harvest.

Seeds are planted in two ways; hearing and saying. When we hear something, a seed is planted within us. When we speak something, a seed is watered within us. The larger the seed grows and develops inside us, the greater it will grow and develop outside of us. That is the reason it is important for us to hear the voice of the Lord spoken. Once we hear it, we then need to hear it again. Why is this? It is so the seed will grow and develop.

The Bible says, "Faith comes by hearing, and hearing by the Word of God" (Romans 10:17). We could also say that faith comes as we hear the voice of the Lord. It is His voice that releases the seed of His Word, which causes faith to arise within our hearts. Then we echo what He said to release our faith. This causes things to change and a new harvest to come forth in our lives.

Every prophetic word spoken over you should be echoed. The seed that God gave you will not produce until you plant it in the ground. It is planted and watered as you repeat it out of your own mouth. So likewise, a seed cannot produce a harvest until it is planted. Your mouth is the tool that God uses to plant and water the seed for His desired harvest to be produced within your life.

Seed for a New Harvest

In 1996, after fifteen years of ministry, the Lord began to speak to my heart concerning planting a church. At first, I thought I was just hearing things. I had no desire to pastor a local church, and I did not consider myself a pastor. At the time, our family was traveling and conducting itinerate ministry. God was blessing us tremendously, and we felt no need to be entangled in the day-to-day responsibilities of caring for a flock. However, God desired fruit to bud in another area of our ministry.

As I previously shared, we traveled to Indianapolis for a conference in which I was ministering. On the Sunday following, I ministered in a local church. After I finished ministering, the pastor of the church called me and my family up to receive prophetic ministry; they immediately began to prophesy concerning planting a local church.

As God's voice was released over our lives, it became the seed that we needed to plant the church that He desired us to pastor. Things began to change in my life because the seed of His voice became the catalyst to bring forth a new desire within my life and ministry. As we took hold of that word, God caused everything to fall into place. The building, leaders, people, and resources came into alignment in a quick manner.

Now, we are a large church with a 32,000 square foot building that seems to be too small at times. The thought of not pastoring is now foreign to me. The seed of the word of the Lord released through His voice produced a harvest of apostolic and pastoral giftings. A harvest was realized that has affected our region and area all because the voice of the Lord was spoken over my life.

God is faithful to give us seed through the release of His voice. However, we must be faithful to plant, water, and nurture the seed so that we see the harvest. It will not happen automatically; we must come into agreement with Him and participate in the process.

Sustenance and Strength

Isaiah continued by saying that the voice of the Lord, the voice of prophecy, will provide bread for the eater. Of course, we know that bread was one of the major components in the diet of those living during the days of Isaiah. They ate it regularly because it sustained them and provided nourishment for their bodies.

Jesus said that man would not live by bread alone but by every word that proceeds from the mouth of God (Matthew 4:4). He made a comparison of bread to the spoken Word of the Lord. Jesus declared that the voice of the Lord has the power to sustain life.

The voice of the Lord is empowered to sustain and strengthen. Inherent within God's voice is the provision and spiritual nourishment needed to cause us to be strong and succeed. This is the reason that Jesus said that physical bread alone would not be enough. While it can give the body strength, it cannot make the spirit of man strong.

All of us encounter situations where we need spiritual strength to prevail in moments of adversity. A protein shake and power snack will not get us through difficult times. However, the voice of the Lord will! When you are going through trials and adversity, the Word will sustain you. Everything else will falter, but the voice of His Word will never fail.

Joseph's Story

We read in the account of Joseph how God spoke to him through several dreams. However, his life took turns that seemed to go opposite of what was revealed to him. His dreams embodied exaltation and promotion, but his life experience seemed to embody everything but the same.

Joseph's envious brothers captured him and threw him into a pit. They lied to their father and said Joseph was killed by a wild animal, but he was actually sold into Egyptian slavery where he became a slave in the house of Potiphar.

Joseph was promoted within the house of Potiphar until the lady of the house decided to sexually assault him, but he ran from her and never obliged her. Through her scorn, she falsely accused Joseph and had him thrown in prison. This was a stark difference from the dream that God gave Joseph.

The Psalmist spoke of Joseph when he declared, "Until the time that his word came: the word of the Lord tried him" (Psalm 105:19, KJV). This verse declares that until the promise was fulfilled within the life of Joseph, his faith in God's promise was put to the test. So, Joseph went through the fire.

God's Spoken Word Fused

This word "tried" literally means to FUSE METAL. Fusion happens when two things come together to make one, and it requires heat to cause the fusion process to take place. You see, when things GET HOT, God will cause the voice of His Word to be FUSED within you so that it becomes a part of you! It causes you and the word of the Lord to become inseparable, which means the devil cannot steal God's promise from you!

When fusing happens, things become stronger. Fusing metals together causes both components to gain strength. Many believers falter because they are not eating their bread and fusing their metal. It is the voice of the Lord that is the bread that we eat and causes the metal of our lives to become strong through spiritual fusing.

It was the word of the Lord that sustained Joseph when he was thrown into the pit. God's promise provided hope to Him when they sold him to Potiphar. It was the voice of the Lord that made him strong when he was thrown into prison based upon a false accusation.

Eventually, God's Word was fulfilled in Joseph's life, and he became the prime minister over all of Egypt. His dream was accomplished when his brothers came and bowed down before him. However, the paramount thing that gives us insight into the purpose for God's voice was stated by Joseph:

> "But as for you, you meant evil against me; but God meant it for good, in order to bring it about as it is this day, to save many people alive. Now therefore, do not be afraid; I will provide for you and your little ones." And he comforted them and spoke kindly to them (Genesis 50:20-21).

We see that God released His voice so Joseph could withstand the pressure and adversity that he experienced and then become a hand of salvation. It was the word that was his bread, and it sustained him through the tough seasons. This ultimately enabled him to be the channel of provision for his entire family. You see, the purpose of the prophetic voice of the Lord is not merely to bring satisfaction and rejoicing in your own life. It is also to be a blessing for others that will be affected by its fulfillment.

We must get over the "this is about me" approach to the prophetic ministry because it defies the very purpose for which God has established His voice within the earth. Instead, we must maintain the understanding that His voice is about His purpose that involves His people.

Empower the Purpose of God

God releases His voice to empower His purpose, which is why we emphasize that God's Word has power. His prophetic voice releases supernatural power for the fulfillment of His divine will and purpose.

When the voice of prophecy is released accurately and concisely, it generates spiritual chain reactions which cause things to happen. The words are sent to accomplish God's intent. It is spoken so that things change and align with the very will and purpose of God. It does what God sends it to do; it does not return void having failed to accomplish something.

It is essential to understand that one of the primary things that God desires to produce when He releases His voice is change. God does not declare things with the expectation that things will remain the same. Instead, He speaks to bring about change and transformation. That is the intent of His spoken voice.

When we hear and receive the prophetic voice of the Lord, it becomes fuel for the purpose of God within our lives. Just like your body needs fuel, so does your spirit man, as does the purpose of God. Just as an automobile cannot depart the garage without fuel, neither can we leave from a stationary spiritual position without spiritual fuel. The voice of the Lord is purposed to be the fuel that we need to embrace and accomplish God's plan.

Everything in life requires fuel—a power source. Many rely on the arm of the flesh and what they can soulishly manipulate. God desires that we depend on Him and His Word rather than the arm of the flesh that will fail. We must see that His voice empowers us to do and achieve His purpose and will. It empowers us to do what the soul and flesh could never accomplish.

Adversity Turned to Victory

"For you shall go out with joy, And be led out with peace; The mountains and the hills Shall break forth into singing before you, And all the trees of the field shall clap their hands" (Isaiah 55:12).

Most of the time, when we allude to a mountain or hill, it references adversity or challenge. Sometimes it may be used to indicate a trial of some sort. Mountains and hills are not generally associated with a place of ease and rest.

Isaiah asserts that the prophetic voice of the Lord being spoken will cause the mountains and hills to break forth into singing. I believe we can see a prophetic picture that the prophet is painting. The word of the Lord causes adverse and challenging situations to turn around. It gives you the power to overcome.

The prophetic voice of the Lord is designed to REVERSE adverse situations. It enables you to overcome the mountains that you face in life. It turns that which was an obstacle into something that sings a song of deliverance.

Some people expect the voice of prophecy to create havoc and difficulty. However, Isaiah says that it will cause a turnaround and breakthrough. Notice, the "mountains and the hills will BREAK FORTH..." My friend, this speaks of breakthrough and victory. This is the declaration of triumph and rejoicing. This is the result of the prophetic voice of the Lord within our lives!

The Voice of Prophecy Produces Breakthrough

My wife, Stacey, and I were married in 1981. In the first seven years of our marriage, we had our most significant financial struggles; I'm sure that is not uncommon among newlyweds. It was unrelenting. Regardless of what we did, it seemed we always had barely enough.

We were faithful givers and faithful to the Lord. We constantly declared God's promises over our finances. We managed our money well (what little we had). We did everything we knew to do and still struggled to live until something happened in a prophetic conference.

A prophet ministered to us and said, "The financial struggle you've experienced in the past will be no more." I remember receiving that prophetic word in 1988. Before the end of the year, our situation had turned around as we experienced a financial breakthrough. Although my salary was less than what it had been years before, God opened doors of supernatural opportunity that caused our income to literally double.

By 1989, we were able to purchase our first home. We began to see a flow of financial provision that we knew existed but had never experienced. The mountains and the hills broke through before us, singing a song of provision.

So, what made the difference? We were not doing anything different than what we had done previously. We were merely in the right place at the right time to receive a right word that made things financially right within our lives! The prophetic voice of the Lord turned things around for us. It produced breakthrough!

In that same year, we were faced with one of the most intense battles we had ever encountered. In February of 1988, we received a prophetic word concerning a daughter being added to our family who would be a dancer in the house of the Lord. The following month, I received three different prophetic exhortations in a conference concerning having another child. One of the words I received indicated that this new addition would be born before the end of the year.

By the end of March of that year, my wife had a positive pregnancy test. We were excited and elated. Unfortunately, the excitement was short-lived. Sometime within the next month, she began to bleed heavily. She went back to the doctor, and a test was done, which revealed a blighted ovum. This happens when a baby is conceived but then dies. The doctor wanted her to go to the hospital and have a D & C procedure.

I was unable to go with my wife to the doctor's appointment, so she called me in tears asking, what she should do. I told her, "We are going to stand and believe the word of the Lord." That night, I laid my hands on her stomach as we prayed together. We declared, "You will live and not die." We did that daily for weeks while she continued to bleed. It was a battle of life and death.

For well over a month, my wife bled daily. However, we continued to declare faithfully what God has spoken prophetically. We echoed the prophetic voice of the Lord over our situation.

Somewhere around the end of May, the bleeding stopped. Stacey rescheduled an appointment at the doctor to see what was taking place. I was able to go to the appointment with her. What a surprise God had prepared for the doctor! He placed the fetal pulse monitor on Stacey's stomach and then jumped back in surprise when the swishing sound of a strong heartbeat was detected. It was glorious.

The voice of the Lord had prevailed and produced a breakthrough in our lives. That year, on December 6th, our daughter, Kayla Denise Gay, was born into this world. The mountains and the hills broke through with singing. The moment of adversity was turned into a breakthrough. The trial of our faith was turned into the gold of a fulfilled promise!

Instead of—Replacement

"Instead of the thorn shall come up the cypress tree,
And instead of the brier shall come up the myrtle tree..."
(Isaiah 55:13).

I love the words "instead of" in this verse. This means that there will be things removed and then replaced because of what God declares prophetically through His voice. Isaiah said instead of the thorn, there would be the cypress tree.

Thorns are things that bring pain. Trees are things that produce shade. Thorns are things that will hurt and cause you to bleed. Trees are things that can protect and ease the situation.

A superficial Bible study will reveal that trees always speak of fruitfulness. The Psalmist said that the blessed man would be like a tree planted by the rivers of water. Jesus said that we are like branches intended to bear fruit. Repeatedly, we see statements made that we are to be trees of righteousness, which speaks of both strength and fruitfulness.

The voice of prophecy comes to cause strength and fruitfulness to abound within your life. It comes to remove the places of dormancy and replace them with life. This is the purpose of the prophetic voice of the Lord. It comes to replace the bad with the good. God desires for you to have an "Instead Of" moment.

The word is spoken so that **instead of** sickness, you will have health. It is declared so that **instead of** poverty, you will have provision. It is prophesied so that **instead of** family problems, you will have family restoration. The voice of the Lord is released to replace the bad fruit with the manifested goodness of God.

We should expect the replacement of the curse with the blessing of the Lord. We should expect the replacing of hell's attack with the victory of heaven. We should expect the replacement of yesterday's pain with the fulfillment of destiny and purpose. The voice of prophecy comes to produce the manifestation of God's blessing within our lives and erase the curse.

10

THE VOICE OF
THE PROPHET

The hand of the LORD came upon me and
brought me out in the Spirit of the LORD,
and set me down in the midst of the valley; and
it was full of bones. Then He caused me to pass
by them all around, and behold, there were very
many in the open valley; and indeed they were
very dry. And He said to me, "Son of man, can
these bones live?" So I answered, "O Lord
GOD, You know." Again He said to me,
"Prophesy to these bones, and say to them, 'O
dry bones, hear the word of the LORD! Thus
says the Lord GOD to these bones: "Surely I
will cause breath to enter into you, and you
shall live. I will put sinews on you and bring
flesh upon you, cover you with skin and put
breath in you; and you shall live. Then you shall
know that I am the LORD."'" So I prophesied
as I was commanded; and as I prophesied,
there was a noise, and suddenly a rattling; and
the bones came together, bone to bone. Indeed,
as I looked, the sinews and the flesh came upon
them, and the skin covered them over; but
there was no breath in them. Also He said to
me, "Prophesy to the breath, prophesy, son of

man, and say to the breath, 'Thus says the Lord GOD: "Come from the four winds, O breath, and breathe on these slain, that they may live."'" So I prophesied as He commanded me, and breath came into them, and they lived, and stood upon their feet, an exceedingly great army. Then He said to me, "Son of man, these bones are the whole house of Israel. They indeed say, 'Our bones are dry, our hope is lost, and we ourselves are cut off!' Therefore prophesy and say to them, 'Thus says the Lord GOD: "Behold, O My people, I will open your graves and cause you to come up from your graves, and bring you into the land of Israel. Then you shall know that I am the LORD, when I have opened your graves, O My people, and brought you up from your graves. I will put My Spirit in you, and you shall live, and I will place you in your own land. Then you shall know that I, the LORD, have spoken it and performed it," says the LORD'" (Ezekiel 37:1-14).

I love this passage of Scripture. In my opinion, this encapsulates the primary purpose for the voice of the prophet in the earth. I am in no way attempting to limit the scope of the prophet to only the things we see in this passage of Scripture, but I believe that this is one of the most concise synopses of what the prophet's ministry is intended to do within the Church today.

There are numerous things that we can observe within this account given by Ezekiel. An entire book could be written on the different elements contained within this narrative.

However, I will highlight some primary points spoken about to bring a greater understanding of the voice of the prophet.

Prophets are important to the heart of God. They are a part of the five-fold ministry that Paul mentions in Ephesians 4:11. They are ascension gifts that were sent to be the continued manifestation of the ministry of Jesus within the earth. Therefore, it is vital that we understand precisely why prophets are still relevant and active in the Church today.

The Voice of Resurrection and Restoration

This entire account begins with the Spirit of the Lord taking the prophet Ezekiel to a valley filled with bones. We often refer to this graveyard as the Valley of Dry Bones. The Lord providentially took Ezekiel to a place that was void of life; the bones were only a reminder of the life that once existed.

God asked the prophet, "Can these bones live?" Ezekiel gave the wise answer, "Lord, you alone know if this can happen." The prophet was not presumptuous to declare if the bones could live or not. He knew his role—just say whatever the Spirit of God told him to speak.

First, let me say that prophets must be careful never to assume that they know what God wants them to speak before He utters it. Failure to do so can produce presumptuous prophetic declarations. It is imperative that prophets posture themselves in the same manner that Ezekiel did; he said nothing until God said to speak.

Once the prophet answered correctly, God gave him a word. He said to Ezekiel, "Prophesy to the bones," and the prophet obeyed God's command. As the voice of the prophet was released, things began to change all around him. This gives us insight into the role of the prophet's voice within the Church today. The Word of the Lord comes to bring change and produce life where death once existed. The voice of the prophet is a voice of resurrection and restoration.

Functioning in the Presence of Its Antithesis

God raises up prophets to speak life where death exists, speak light where darkness abounds, and speak love where hatred and strife are prevalent. The voice of the prophet is not released to evaluate and critique the surroundings. Anyone can make a commentary on present situations and conditions. It never takes a rocket scientist to talk about problems that are evident, but it requires someone with an anointed word to release the will of God in the earth through a prophetic declaration. This is what Ezekiel did. The voice of the prophet is released to bring change and transformation.

Think about this for a moment. In the beginning, when God created the heavens and the earth, He stepped out into the darkness and said, "Let there be light." God did not comment about how dark it was everywhere. He spoke His will and desire. Likewise, God raises up the prophet's voice to echo His will and purpose, not give commentary on contemporary happenings.

This is exactly what Ezekiel did. He declared life where death existed. He spoke to bones and commanded them to hear the Word of the Lord. Ezekiel did not offer commentary on the present condition of the bones. Instead, he specifically spoke the word that God told Him to speak. In the middle of a graveyard absent of life, he prophesied to bones and told them to live.

We must recognize that the voice of the prophet is intended for unfavorable conditions. Many want to prophesy in conditions of life, fertility, and fruitfulness. However, God raises up prophetic voices to release life where death is prevailing. He anoints prophets to speak in less than desirable situations so that transformation and change will be realized.

The voice of the prophet is specifically purposed to reverse circumstances and situations. It is intended to bring change into present conditions. **Prophetic anointings and giftings are divinely released to function in the presence of its antithesis.** For instance, the healing anointing is created to operate where sickness is present. The anointing for deliverance is intended to manifest where there is demonic infiltration. Likewise, the prophet's anointing is designed to operate where there is no life, light, direction, or understanding.

God told Ezekiel to speak life where death was in abundance. The voice of the prophet comes to confront and change the thing that is in full manifestation. Prophets speak things contrary to what is seen so that change will transpire by the authority of God's spoken Word.

Prophets "Forthtell"

God renamed Abram and called him Abraham. Abraham means *father of many nations*. So even though he had no children, God called him Abraham, father of many nations. God calls those things which are not in existence as though they already existed.

147

With this understanding, it only stands to reason that the voice of the prophet will speak and prophesy of things not yet in existence; this is part of the nature of prophecy. If it existed, then it would merely be a commentary on the present situation. However, the prophet's voice comes to "forthtell" what is to happen and take place. It does not come merely to foretell but forthtell. Prophets are not predicting things like a palm reader or soothsayer; rather, they are speaking and releasing God's will through His creative Word.

It is in the middle of destruction that God will anoint prophets to speak restoration and wholeness. It is in the places of disaster that God will anoint prophets to declare renewal and repair. In the place of tragedy and defeat, God will anoint prophets to speak triumph and victory. God releases life where dry bones once existed.

SHALAM!

On October 10, 2018, Hurricane Michael, a Category 5 tropical cyclone hit the panhandle of Florida. The eye of the storm that packed 165 mph winds and gusts near 200 mph went directly over the eastern part of Bay County, Florida. It just so happened that the eye of the storm passed straight over my home and the church building where I pastor. Our entire area was devastated. It looked as if an atomic bomb had exploded and leveled most things in a radius of 20 miles or more. It was terrifying and heartbreaking.

My wife and our family evacuated during the storm and retreated to Orlando. During the storm, we watched on television as it traveled its path. A category five hurricane causes catastrophic damage (only four category five storms have ever hit the U.S. since 1851). So, all we could do was pray, wait, and believe for the best.

When pictures came back of the sheer devastation, the Lord gave me a prophetic word for our congregation and the people of the area. The Lord spoke to me the Scripture found in Joel 2:25, "I will restore to you..." I shared the word in a video on Facebook and encouraged our people. I still have very vivid memories of that moment.

At the time I gave the word, I did not know everything that God meant when I spoke it. Often, prophets and prophetic voices can speak but not fully comprehend what God is saying. Paul said, "For we know in part and we prophesy in part" (1 Corinthians 13:9).

Later, I did a word study specifically on the word "restore," which is the Hebrew word *SHALAM*. This word is the root word for *shalom*. When the word *shalam* is used and translated as "restore," it typically means to have a greater amount than you had previously, more than you had before. This was quickened to me by the Lord, and I started declaring that we would have more than we had before. Our entire church body started using the word "SHALAM" and saying that we would have more than we had before.

As time went by, there were testimonies of people who received large settlements and payouts that resulted in their homes ending up in a better condition than before the hurricane. The testimonies poured in from people concerning restoration of their properties. Their situations on the other side of the storm were better than before the devastation. Many companies and private contractors made more financially than they had in the history of their businesses. God fulfilled His Word; He did what He said He would do.

Our church was not only able to repair and restore the damage, but we were able to eliminate the remaining debt on the building. I was able to repair the damage to my home and have funds left over for improvements. God did exactly what He said, and we had more than we had before. Hallelujah!

While our region is still in a time of rebuilding and reconstruction, it has been amazing to watch the Word of the Lord be fulfilled within our lives. His Word brought forth a resurrection. His Word caused the dry bones to live.

The Voice of the Prophet Brings Structure

Prophets are an extension and part of the hand of God that is used to build the Church. They come to contribute to the building of the skeletal structure of the body of Christ. We see a picture of this in the narrative given by Ezekiel when he said that as he prophesied, the bones came together, bone to bone.

We know that bones comprise the skeletal structure of our physical bodies. Bones are the foundation upon which the rest of the body is built. No one can exist without their bones being properly connected. There must be a proper skeletal structure for the muscles and tendons to be attached and for the organs to be housed. Without a skeletal structure provided by proper connection of bones, we would be a pile of mush, and our human existence would cease.

Just as bones within our bodies are the foundation of our existence, the voice of the prophet is released to establish the very foundations of the functioning Church. This is not to equate the prophet's voice to that of canonized Scripture that we have in the Bible. However, it is important to understand that the prophet is a foundational ministry in the body of Christ, and without it, the Church will only be a pile of mush. The voice of the prophet is needed to help position the bones and bring skeletal strength to the body of Christ.

Walking Uprightly

The skeletal structure of our natural bodies gives us the ability to walk upright. Likewise, one of the roles of the prophet's voice in the earth is to cause the body of Christ to walk uprightly. Prophetic voices should always push Christians toward holy living. They should herald the call for the Church to walk in righteousness and cease sinful behavior. Any prophet that encourages sinful living and debauchery is a false voice— a false prophet.

In the Old Testament, God anointed prophets to call the nation of Israel back to a place of consecration and holy living. They would declare the penalty of sin and the reward of walking uprightly. The manner that the king and the nation responded to the voice of the prophet would then determine their outcome, whether there would be penalty or blessing.

I personally believe that the prophet's voice is not established in the Church to speak spiritual niceties. Instead, it is there to confront the issues that need to be changed in the lives of believers.

Many times, when we speak of the purpose of prophecy, we say that it is to edify, exhort, and comfort because this is what

Paul told the church at Corinth. Part of the process of edification is to build a structure. Prophets speak the word of the Lord to produce an upright walk of righteousness in the body of Christ. Edification does not mean there will never be a word of rebuke. It means that what is necessary for us to walk uprightly is being spoken so we will not fall. Prophecy is intended to accomplish this in the life of believers.

Again, this aspect of the prophet's voice is connected with establishing the skeletal structure of the body of Christ. It is that structure that gives us the ability to live holy and walk uprightly.

When things are not structured correctly within the lives of believers, they will fall. They will miss the mark and do things that are unfitting for believers to do. However, when there is a strong spiritual skeletal structure in our lives, we will be strong and overcome the tactics and strategies of the enemy.

Protection and Safety

Another thing that our skeleton does is provide protection and safety. The bones in our upper body protect vital organs that are necessary for living. The slight knocks we experience in life could potentially kill us without our skeletal structure.

It is important to understand that the voice of the prophet is not purposed to control or manipulate. However, it is released to prevent us from being harmed. There is great protection that is afforded when we heed an accurate prophetic declaration over our lives. Listening and adhering to a prophetic warning can sometimes be the difference between life and death.

The apostle Paul had a prophetic sensing about his journey on a ship. He warned the commanding officer that great danger was awaiting them if they set sail. The commander refused to listen to the prophetic warning. As a result, the ship and everything on it were lost at sea. All the passengers were saved, but Paul made sure that the commander knew that he should have listened and given heed to the prophetic warning.

Paul was given prophetic insight, a spiritual sensing, concerning things that would occur if there was no course correction. He was faithful to give the word, though the commanding officer rejected it. The refusal of Paul's word and sensing resulted in great loss.

Believers must realize that the voice of the prophet, as it functions to give skeletal structure to the Church, will protect believers from impending harm if they take heed. It will act as part of our spiritual skeleton that protects us both spiritually and naturally from the attacks of the enemy. Embracing the voice of the prophet is necessary for us to secure the protection that God promises for all areas of our lives.

Order and Coordination

Another thing that happens because of proper skeletal structure is that it makes way for structured coordinated movement. The foundational element within your body that gives you the ability to move is your skeletal structure; all muscles and tendons attach to the skeleton. Anyone who has ever experienced a detached muscle or tendon can tell you that proper movement and function are forfeited because of this type of injury. If muscles are not attached to the bones, then there can be no coordinated movement.

Those who fail to embrace the voice of the prophet will forfeit coordinated movement in their churches and personal lives. They may possess other elements that allow temporary external success, but there will ultimately be chaos without proper structure. Prophetic voices keep things on the right track and bring proper coordination to the body of Christ.

Divine order is not merely the byproduct of the implementation of natural organizational skills. While these skills may be instrumental, establishing God's order requires the spiritual reception of God's blueprint for our lives, individually and corporately. These things are known and learned through spiritual discernment. We derive principles from the written Word of God, the personal witness of the Holy Spirit, and prophetic voices that speak specific direction for us individually.

God's Voice is Unique and Specific

Just as no two human bodies are identical, neither are two spiritual bodies. What may work for one may not work for the other. What blesses one may not bless the other. We share many things in common, but there are many things that are specific to us individually. That is why God has placed the indwelling voice of the Holy Spirit and prophetic voices in our lives. Together they give us specifics concerning God's blueprint for the spiritual structure of our lives, families, churches, and any other endeavor in which we may be involved.

God created us individually and uniquely; He did not clone us. We are all individually a "one off," meaning we are originals— not a copy. There is no one else on the planet that is identical to you. A person's call and purpose may be similar to that of another, yet it is never identical. We are all part of the same family with the same Father, but we all look and function somewhat differently from each other.

Understanding these truths will help us realize the importance of the voice of the prophet. It is key to individually giving us the structure we need to function in the Church. It will equally help the structuring and functioning of the local church within the body of Christ at large.

Bone to Bone

When Ezekiel prophesies, the first thing he specifically mentions is the bones that were once scattered come together. The voice of the prophet will cause people to get connected. Accurate prophetic voices will cause the individual members of the church to connect rather than disconnect. If anyone claiming to be a prophet speaks things that cause division and disconnection within the church, they should be avoided because they do not represent an accurate manifestation of the prophetic ministry.

The very first thing that Ezekiel's prophecy accomplished was bringing the bones together. Prophets gather, not scatter. Prophetic utterances should point people toward ministry and function within the parameters of the gathering of believers. The voice of the prophet is not to disconnect members from the church and get them connected to the prophet. True and accurate prophets do not point people toward themselves; they point toward the Church and its advancement in promoting the gospel and the kingdom of God.

Accurate prophetic words will never encourage people to be the "Lone Ranger" and disconnect from their church body. They will not tell them to ignore spiritual counsel received from their pastors or leaders. However, it will rebuke people who have disconnected. It will encourage those sitting on the sidelines to put their hand to the plow and start using what God has given them within their local church body. Prophetic utterances are intended to cause the bones to come together.

The Voice of the Prophet Brings Unity

The voice of the prophet is designed to bring unity to the Church. It is a rallying cry for the body of Christ to come together under the banner of the name of Jesus. The prophetic voice is to unify those from all walks of life who confess Jesus as Lord and have made a dedication of heart to Him. Prophets are not placed in the Church to bring disunity, disorder, and disconnection. It is accurate to say that those who do such things and call themselves prophets are speaking inaccurately and may not be true prophets of the Lord.

During the year 2020, there was a tremendous amount of controversy surrounding prophetic utterances and the prophet's ministry. Many accurately prophesied that it was a year of clear vision. However, that word manifested in ways that none of us expected. Unfortunately, we saw a side of the body of Christ that was not pretty. The underbelly of the Church was exposed as God brought to light issues that needed to be addressed.

Unfortunately, a great deal of division was produced within the Church that was linked to prophets and things they prophesied during these happenings. Not all prophets were involved, but there were enough that it caused disagreement within churches, relationships, and friendships. I will devote greater clarity to these things in my next book, *Voices of Deception*. However, it is safe to say God is not involved in dividing His people over social and political opinions of the day that will be a distant memory in another decade.

Rally around Jesus

The voice of the prophet is intended to rally people around the name above every name, Jesus. It is not purposed to rally people around a man, a pet doctrine, a single local church, or a political leader. The prophet's voice causes bones to come together, not separate!

If prophets are not bringing people together, then we have reason to question the validity of their word. If they are causing strife, division, and discord, we should at least take a step back and evaluate what they have spoken. This is the biblical thing to do which protects the body of Christ.

Psalm 133 declares that it is good and pleasant for brothers to dwell together in unity. It proceeds to say that it is like the anointing oil that flowed down the beard and garments of Aaron. It furthermore says the place of unity is where God commands His blessing to be in manifestation.

If God says that His anointing and blessing will flow where unity exists, then the voice of the prophet is intended to release and instigate it in the body of Christ. His voice should never divide and produce strife. It is antithetical to what God desires to be in manifestation. It opposes the very will and purpose of God if it genders strife, hatred, gossip, and malice.

When Ezekiel prophesied, bones came together. When he prophesied, they assembled in their proper place. When Ezekiel prophesied, the scattered bones gathered. The voice of the prophet should do the same.

Strength and Function

As Ezekiel continued to prophesy, muscles and flesh came upon the bones that reassembled. Tendons and organs reappeared as the things necessary for a body to function were recreated. This speaks specifically of strength and function within the body of Christ that is to be produced through the voice of the prophet. The Word of the Lord is intended to not only bring things together but also equip us with the strength and facilities to accomplish His purpose within the earth.

Just as muscles need a skeleton to connect to a body, the skeleton needs the muscles to give it the ability and strength to function. The skeleton (bones) provides the structure for function while the muscles provide the strength to function. We need both to succeed in our mission and advance the kingdom of God.

It is interesting to note that Paul specifically compared the Church to a natural body. In his letter to the Corinthian church, he emphasized that every part of the body was necessary and had a unique function. We could equally say that every bone is necessary, and every muscle has a unique function. Some members of the Church provide structure, while others will provide strength and power. Both are necessary for the fulfillment of God's will. They are designed to be connected and working together to bring spiritual mobility and function in the earth.

Muscles Are Developed

Muscles are not fully matured at birth or through the growing process alone; they must be developed. I have biceps just like Mr. Universe. However, his biceps are greatly developed through exercise and use, while mine have only been slightly developed through sitting at a computer like I am at this writing.

Those who consistently work out at a gymnasium will have their muscles tone, fit, and developed. Those who use their muscles in a more limited way will have less developed muscles. Both groups of people have the same muscles; however, through exercise and use, one group will be stronger than the other.

The voice of the prophet may provide you with spiritual muscle, but you will still need to develop that muscle. There may be an articulation and bestowment of gifts, but those will need to be exercised so they will become full-grown.

The prophet's voice is an invitation for you to become what God has called you to be. It is an exhortation to grow, mature, and blossom into the fullness that God has prepared for your life and ministry. The prophetic voice is not a guarantee that something will happen, rather an opportunity to partner with the Lord to see it happen, to see His will manifested in the earth.

Muscles Must Remain Attached

I want to emphasize once again that muscles must be attached to the body to give it strength. Once a muscle or tendon becomes detached from the bone, it can no longer function in the way that it was created to operate. You can be the strongest man in the world, but the moment your muscles and tendons become detached, you will cease to be able to do anything.

There are many believers today who become involved in a local church; they become attached. As they begin to exercise and use their gifts, they grow and develop. Many people are blessed and edified by their ministry. For various reasons, many of these people later detach themselves from the body. They were once useful and productive, yet because of detachment, they become useless.

Some of them detach themselves because they do not like the perceived limitation the skeletal structure places upon them. However, they fail to realize that without that structure in place, they would be able to do nothing.

The prophetic voice of the Lord will not only recreate the muscle, but it will cause it to be attached in the right place. That is the role of the voice of the prophet. It is not to create individualistic spiritual islands that are nowhere connected. Instead, the prophet's voice will point toward Christ and His body, the Church.

The Organs of the Church

As Ezekiel prophesied to the dry bones, human bodies were recreated. The bones came together from various places; muscles and tendons came on the bones. All the necessary components needed for a human body to live were manifested in front of the prophet.

All human bodies must have the necessary organs. We must have a heart, brain, lungs, kidneys, skin, and liver to sustain life. The organs within our body are the things that keep our blood flowing and prevents us from dying. Without them, we cannot live.

Every organ within our body has a specific function. Each one has a particular location within the human anatomy. The kidneys are not in the skull, and the brain is not in the rib cage. There is a designated location and function for every organ in our body. Any organ that is not functioning or is out of place can cause problems for the entire body.

I knew a man who had digestive issues and problems breathing. He went to the doctor to be examined because it was causing him great distress. His doctor did a variety of tests and determined that his problem was caused by his stomach being elevated up into his chest. The fact that one organ in his body was out of place caused problems with other organs, particularly his heart and lungs.

Every organ within the body of Christ must be positioned and functioning properly for the whole body to be at its optimum. When organs are out of place, things will go awry. When spiritual organs are not working, the body can suffer and ultimately die. Therefore, it is imperative that every organ in the body is aware of its role, function, and placement for things to run smoothly.

The voice of the prophet plays a key role in revealing the function and placement of every organ within the Church. It gives guidance to how things are to flow together for the advancement of God's purpose.

Not for Personal Validation

It is important to understand that the majority of organs are not seen, yet life cannot exist without them. An organ exists solely for the entire body and not for itself. My heart exists exclusively to pump blood throughout my physical body. It is not seen, nor does it seek glory. It does its job 24/7 knowing that to some degree, I take it for granted. For the most part, I do not think about my heart. I do not thank it every day and tell it what a great job it is doing. I do not compliment it on its faithfulness to continue beating.

The same thing could be said about my kidneys, liver, pancreas, lungs, and brain. They do what they were created to do. They are not seen, and we give them little to no attention, but they continue to function for the sake of the entire body. They do their job consistently without any commendation from the tongue in my mouth.

Likewise, the prophet's voice is not for the purpose of telling any of us how great we are. It speaks of the greatness of the Lord and His purpose for us as functioning members of the Church. The voice of the prophet seeks to identify and position organs properly within the body of Christ. It does not seek to exalt a particular organ within the body. It aims to exalt Jesus and His purpose within the earth. It gives direction to the organs concerning function and position.

Many times, in my younger days of ministry, I desired prophetic ministry so I could be validated. I wanted to hear from the prophet how God approved of me and planned on using me in the future. Not only did I want to hear it, but I wanted everyone around me to hear it too. I wanted them to know that I was "chosen." These were things I did in my immaturity. I made the voice of the prophet about ME, while God intended it to be about HIM.

I recognize that prophetic words will at times affirm us. I know that there is a measure of validation we can receive from the voice of the prophet. However, that is not its primary purpose, nor is it the source from which we should derive these things. Our personal time in the Word and communion with the Lord is where we should receive our affirmation and validation.

An improper approach to the voice of the prophet can cause one to miss the most important things being declared. The prophetic ministry is released for the purpose of articulating and clarifying function and purpose. It is not to exalt one man in the eyes of other men. Its purpose is not to be a spiritual pat on the back to make us feel better about ourselves. Approaching the voice of the prophet in this manner will cause the reverse effect of its intention. Instead of being placed correctly within the body, we become detached because we made the word about us rather than His purpose. Think about it!

I have said repeatedly that anytime we approach something without understanding its purpose, we will misuse it and fail to receive the full benefit. It is imperative to understand that God anoints prophets to speak and declare His will and purpose, not commend the great job we are doing. It is not for personal adulation or affirmation. He anoints prophets so that His divine purpose will be clearly articulated and the members of the body of Christ will function correctly.

An Exceeding Great and Mighty Army

The last thing that God commands Ezekiel to prophesy is for the lifeless bodies to breathe. The prophet did as God commanded him, which resulted in the rising of an exceedingly great and mighty army.

Ultimately, the voice of the prophet is for the purpose of raising up a mighty spiritual army of believers. The prophet's voice is not designed to speak flowery words so that we can sit at home and think well of ourselves. Instead, it is released so that believers will come into a knowledge of their divine destiny and arise to fulfill it. The prophet's voice is a call for the army of God to assemble and move forward to take territory for the kingdom of God.

All armies are composed of people with unique individual responsibilities. However, they all share a common purpose: to protect their nation and fight their enemies. Everything that individual soldiers do will point toward a corporate objective. Likewise, everything that individual soldiers in the army of the Lord do will point toward the corporate purpose of making the Church strong and overcoming satan.

Soldiers who cannot embrace corporate purpose will cease to be soldiers. They become the ones that are selfish and motivated by vainglory. They cause problems in the ranks and ultimately affect the other soldiers negatively. They are bad for morale and cause their unit to experience decreased productivity. As it is in the natural, so it is in the spiritual.

God Had One Intention

From the time Ezekiel arrives at the Valley of Dry Bones until he leaves, God had one intention. His plan was to raise up an army. The voice of the prophet is not purposed to flatter the individual members of the body or the individual soldiers that makeup the army. Instead, he prophesies to gather, assemble, recreate, initiate, and rejuvenate an army that before was nothing but scattered bones in a graveyard. The word of the Lord resurrected and gave life to what was previously dead!

An army functions because there is rank and order. If the soldiers were free to do as they pleased, there would be chaos and confusion. An army has generals, commanders, and soldiers that function by rank and order. Therefore, when someone enlists in the military, there are certain freedoms they possessed while a civilian that they forfeit for the sake of their mission. If the General gives a soldier an assignment, they do it without question. If the Commander tells them to move forward, they do so. Regardless of what they may want to do individually, they subjugate themselves to the word of their commanding officer.

In a similar manner, Jesus is the Head and General of His army. There are commanding officers throughout, which we refer to as five-fold ministry gifts. This consists of the apostle, prophet, evangelist, pastor, and teacher. Then there are elders and leaders under these that God has established. The intent is not to promote hierarchy but rather order that must be present for the army of the Lord to function.

The voice of the prophet will reinforce rank and order. It will support the order and structure of the Church. To do anything differently would be self-destructive and counterproductive for the body of Christ. The prophet's voice brings divine order within the manifestation of ministry, not promoting a spiritual free-for-all.

When we understand the purpose for the voice of the prophet, the Church will advance. The prophetic ministry is not designed to advance a personality, rather the kingdom of God. The accurate demonstration of the voice of the prophet will do that; it will promote the kingdom of God and the name of the Lord. Let us embrace the voice of the prophet and see the kingdom of God advance.

11

PROPHETIC PURITY
AND INTEGRITY

Do not quench the Spirit. Do not despise
prophecies. Test all things; hold fast what is
good. Abstain from every form of evil (1
Thessalonians 5:19-22).

The prophetic ministry is one of the most powerful aspects of
the voice of the Holy Spirit within the Church. It possesses
great ability to build up and bless the members of the body of
Christ. Personally, it has benefited me, my family, and our
church body more than any other manifestation of the Holy
Spirit. I greatly appreciate and love the gift of prophecy.

The apostle Paul said that we are to covet to prophesy. This is
something only said about the gift of prophecy. There is no
other manifestation gift of the Spirit that we are told to covet
and earnestly desire. It is also the only gift declared that
everyone can manifest. First Corinthians 14:31 states, "For you
may all prophesy one by one..." (MKJV).

Paul said to refrain from quenching the manifestations of the
Holy Spirit and never despise the function of the gift of
prophecy. We must always maintain gratitude for this powerful
gift that Jesus placed in the body of Christ. It should never be

disesteemed, slighted, or ignored. On the contrary, we should embrace and cherish its operation and function within the Church.

Test the Spirits

Just as we are commanded to embrace prophetic ministry, we are also admonished to test, judge, and evaluate it. Every prophetic word given should be evaluated by both the leaders in a church and those who hear the word declared. This is a vital aspect of prophetic ministry that is often ignored. In our zealousness to receive a fresh word from the Lord, we can never ignore the necessity to test it.

> Beloved, do not believe every spirit, but test the spirits, whether they are of God; because many false prophets have gone out into the world (1 John 4:1).

John said that we are to test the spirits whether they are of God. This means that it is possible for someone to put "thus says the Lord" at the end of their declaration, and it proves to be inaccurate or false. John says that there are many false prophets in the world. We could also say many false voices are in operation today. This is not to say that someone who prophesies something inaccurately is a false prophet. However, we must be aware that they do exist and that prophets can give a false word.

Every prophetic utterance must be proven and tested. The first test is that of the written Word of God; all prophecies must align with the Bible. If it fails to pass that test, then it must be considered an illegitimate voice. Prophetic words contrary to biblical principle, precept, and purpose must be discarded regardless of who speaks.

Prophetic words must agree with the words of Jesus in letter and spirit. As was already stated, the testimony of Jesus is the spirit of prophecy. If the words spoken are contrary to what Jesus said, then it must be refused. It must be deemed illegitimate.

Words must also be evaluated based on the witness of the spirit. Does the word bear witness with your spirit, or is there a sensing that it was not on target? Asking these questions is not an indictment against the individual delivering the word. These things are meant to protect the ones hearing and receiving the prophetic word.

Paul said that we are to test all things (everything prophesied) and hold fast to what is good (receive it and believe it). Once a word is tested and proven to be accurate, then it should be believed and received. We should treasure it, embrace it, confess it, and fight the devil with it!

Words for the Battle

Prophetic words are released within our lives to give us ammunition against satan. The apostle Paul told Timothy to war a good warfare with the prophecies that he had received. God's prophetic words spoken over our lives are like arrows in the hands of a warrior. They will strike the heart of the enemy and render him powerless. Hallelujah!

In the natural realm, every weapon that ever ends up on the battlefield is first tested. Firearms, tanks, aircraft, missiles, etc., will go through rigorous tests before they ever show up in live combat. These things must be proven first. It would be unwise to mass-produce anything that had not been tested.

The reason for all the testing is that it may be the difference between life and death. If the weapon fails in combat, people will die. If it cannot stand up to the rigors of a test, it will never succeed on the field of battle. The test is not meant to disqualify; it is intended to ensure. It is meant to protect the lives of those who are going to be using the weaponry. It is to ensure their safety.

Likewise, prophetic words are tested to ensure they are accurate and will still maintain their integrity when someone is going through the fire. A false word gives you no protection and will falter in the time of adversity. An inaccurate word cannot be used as a sword against the enemy. It will be like Styrofoam™ rather than forged steel. There is a big difference.

No Doubting, Just Proving

Proving does not mean doubting. Evaluating and scrutinizing a prophetic word does not mean that you doubt it. Testing the word means you are obedient to a biblical command that was given by the apostle Paul. Proving something to be accurate or inaccurate will be a life-saving measure later on down the road.

Paul said to hold fast to what is good and abstain from every form of evil. The Greek word translated as "evil" means hurtful. Paul is saying that we are to receive the words that will build up and bless but refuse questionable prophetic declarations that have the potential to hurt us and others.

I believe Paul is also exhorting us to minister in such a way that people are not harmed. We must be faithful to steward the gifts we have received so that it hurts no one. This means that biblical parameters should be implemented, practiced, and followed. The prophetic ministry is powerful. It has great ability to build up the Church, but used incorrectly, it can harm.

Electricity has the power to do many wonderful life-giving things. However, if it is mishandled, it can kill someone—the greater the power, the greater the parameters. The prophetic ministry is the same way. Great anointing does not mean that biblical parameters are discarded; it is the exact opposite.

Preventing Prophetic Confusion

I have been involved in the prophetic ministry to some degree or another for forty years. I am not a novice and was mentored by some of the most knowledgeable and wisest leaders within the prophetic movement. So, I want to share things I have learned over the years that need to be implemented and practiced to maintain purity and integrity in the prophetic ministry—the voice of prophecy. These are things that will help prevent confusion and error.

The apostle Paul placed numerous guidelines on the ministry of the gifts of the Spirit, specifically the gift of prophecy. While this gift has the greatest ability to bless and edify those within the Church, it can also damage if not handled properly. Therefore, I want to give some practical guidelines that should be practiced so that the prophetic ministry will maintain its integrity. I will only take time to give a brief explanation of each point.

1. Maintain a proper understanding of the biblical purpose for prophecy along with biblical parameters governing the prophetic ministry.

Paul said that prophecy comes to edify, exhort, and comfort the body of Christ (1 Corinthians 14:3). This is the primary function of prophetic utterances within the Church. If what we are prophesying is failing to do this, we must question its validity.

Prophecy is not intended to be a "crystal ball" to merely see into the future. The prophetic ministry is not placed in the body of Christ for entertainment purposes. The voice of the Lord in manifestation is not purposed to intrigue and fascinate people; it is designed to build and bless the Church.

Any prophetic ministry should be done within the parameters clearly stated in Paul's writings. I will not go into detail as we have already discussed some of them. I encourage for all prophecies to be recorded. If you receive a prophetic word, transcribe it, and meditate upon it. If you fail to understand it, seek counsel from your pastor or overseer. Do what Paul instructed us to do, prove all things and hold fast to what is good.

2. Emphasis should be placed on the character of those who are ministering prophetically.

Inaccurate prophetic words alone do not make someone a false prophet. Rather, it is failure to exhibit the character of Christ coupled with wrong motives. Prophetic ministers should be humble and willing to receive instruction and correction. Arrogance and pride are unacceptable qualities in those who minister prophetically. Accountability is important for all who prophesy.

Prophets who operate without the character of Christ bring reproach on the body of Christ. That character starts with loving people and acting appropriately. A tremendous amount can be said about manifesting these qualities that we will not take time to address. However, prophets and prophetic people should live a holy life before God and be unspotted by the world. Nothing brings reproach on the Church like those who preach and prophesy but fail to live a lifestyle fitting and worthy of their call.

3. Maintain a humble spirit and remain teachable.

It is important for all believers who operate in any spiritual gift to allow those who are seasoned to speak into their lives. Most of the individuals that I have witnessed make the biggest mistakes are the ones who were unteachable. Those who refuse to receive instruction will manifest error. Any spiritual gift that God bestows upon us should be received with grace and humility rather than pride and arrogance. A haughty spirit always precedes a fall.

Anyone who prophesies should be submitted to spiritual oversight. They should allow for evaluation of what they are declaring and how they are doing it without being hypersensitive to critique. Prophetic believers need to invite constructive criticism concerning the way and manner that they operate within their gift and then make the necessary adjustments. Spiritual mentoring is necessary for anyone who is called and anointed. We see this practiced with Moses and Joshua, Elijah and Elisha, and Paul and Timothy, to name a few. Those who fail to embrace this principle ultimately hurt other members of the body of Christ.

4. Avoid captivation with sensational experiences (angelic visitations, being taken to heaven, heavenly scrolls being opened, out-of-body experiences, etc.).

We must understand that these sorts of things are not designed to be the norm for everyday Christian life. While these supernatural encounters are biblically legitimate, they are not normal everyday experiences for believers.

Sensational and supernatural experiences are not designed to be used to establish what we believe and practice. They are usually given for the spiritual insight of those who are the recipients, not direction for the entire body of Christ. A strange experience does not equate to being a heavenly revelation. Fascination with these types of things can open the door for deception through fabrication and conjuring.

5. Understand the difference between a declaration of faith vs. a word of prophecy.

As believers, we are given authority to speak and declare the promise of God. However, putting "thus says the Lord" at the end of a declaration of faith is not equivalent to prophecy. We must not ascribe the name of the Lord to the desire of our hearts. Yes, we should make bold declarations of faith. No, we should not ascribe them to be the prophetic voice of the Lord. Our personal desire to see something manifested is not equivalent to the prophetic voice of the Lord. So, the Lord's name should not be ascribed to it.

6. Refrain from prophesying from positional indoctrination.

We should never merely state our doctrinal position and put "thus says the Lord" at the end. This not only applies to biblical indoctrination, but also cultural, social, and political indoctrination. Our conviction about the truth of our position does not merit it to be prophesied in the name of the Lord. A prophetic word should be a fresh flow of spiritual water, not a regurgitation of a soulish persuasion.

Over the last decade, we have seen the growth of fascination over conspiracy narratives. Some believers even consider them prophetic in nature. Unfortunately, there are those who recite these theories while ascribing the name of the Lord to them. The testimony of Jesus is the spirit of prophecy; the declaration of theories is not.

One of the indicators of spiritual immaturity is the inability to separate that which is soulish from that which is spiritual. The conviction of something being true from naturally attained knowledge does not warrant it being prophesied. We must check ourselves so that we are not merely uttering an intellectual indoctrination with God's name ascribed at the end.

7. Never permit political allegiances or leanings to influence prophetic ministry.

The prophet Nathan presumptuously told King David to build the temple because of his loyalty to the king. He had to return and tell David that he was wrong. His loyalty and allegiance to the king caused him to err.

Understand that prophets are called to confront earthly systems, not align with them, and tell them what they want to hear. The only prophets in the Bible that we see operating with blind allegiance were the false prophets of Baal. Samuel confronted Saul, as Nathan did David. On the other hand, the prophets of Baal only spoke good things to Ahab and Jezebel, regardless of their ungodly conduct.

There is a thin line between allegiance and political idolatry. We must make sure that our spiritual wells remain pure and prevent any idols from entering our hearts. I believe it to be inappropriate for one to prophesy that a candidate they support is the person to elect or is God's chosen. There is too much room for error and fleshly influence.

8. Refrain from competition to see who will have the next great spiritual revelation.

The desire for acceptance, recognition, and fame can cause ministers to say and prophesy questionable things. Engaging in a race to see who will have the next powerful prophetic revelation and be recognized is a trap the enemy uses to ensnare prophetic ministers in error. I have witnessed some ministers get caught up in the "dueling banjos" ministry syndrome. This is the road that leads to inaccurate words. Attempting to "out-prophesy" another minister is dangerous and can bring harm to the body of Christ as words are fabricated from a heart with incorrect motives.

9. Do not put dates and times on prophetic words.

This was done repeatedly concerning COVID and the 2020 election. Being specific in an attempt to give the appearance of pinpointed accuracy only brings reproach on the prophetic ministry when things do not transpire. Putting dates and times on prophetic words will not make them valid or accurate; the reverse is usually true. Most prophets do not miss it in the content of the word but the date they stamp on it.

10. Prophets are never to claim infallibility.

Prophets can prophesy soulishly or presumptuously and miss it for a variety of reasons. I tell anyone prophesying within our local church that all prophecies are subject to spiritual evaluation. Any prophet unwilling to allow their word to be scrutinized should refrain from prophesying. Prophetic accuracy is more important than the exercising of someone's gift.

No prophet should ever say that a prophecy is true solely because they prophesied it, even if a hundred prophets said the same thing. Neither should they give guarantees that their words will take place. Once someone claims infallibility with statements such as, "I know that I heard from God, so don't question me," then it is impossible to obey biblical directives in the way of judging and evaluating prophetic utterances.

While prophetic terminology can be the reason that some things do not take place immediately, a prophet should not use that as an explanation to claim they are right when something is obviously inaccurate. It is inappropriate to double down on an inaccurate prophetic word.

It is possible for someone to prophesy something accurately, and it never takes place. This is because every prophetic word is conditional, whether conditions are stated at the time the word is given. However, it is much better for prophets to operate in humility and at least concede they are not infallible and that there is the possibility of them speaking something presumptuously. This is not an admission to missing it, but rather that they could unintentionally declare something inaccurately.

11. Avoid prophetic words concerning political elections.

I can remember discussions in my early days of prophetic mentorship concerning election prophecies. While it was never strictly forbidden, it was discouraged. The conclusion was that elections are reflections of the will of man, not necessarily the will of God. It was emphasized if you were going to prophesy concerning an election result, you should make sure you heard correctly because of potential confusion and reproach it could produce. A reflection on our most recent election reveals that truth.

12. Never attempt to control or manipulate through prophetic utterances.

Prophecy is not for the purpose of controlling or manipulating people to do things. Statements such as "if you don't believe that my prophetic word is right, then you shouldn't be in the pulpit," or "if you are not contending for what I prophesied, then you don't believe the prophets" are examples of using the prophetic in attempts to control through shame. These kinds of statements seek to use supposed prophetic words to control what people believe and do. Using a prophetic utterance as a means to manipulate through shaming is always inappropriate. This is ungodly and should be avoided.

One of the many wonderful things I was taught in my early days of prophetic mentorship was just to deliver the word. We were instructed to give the word of the Lord and then leave it to the recipient to make application of that word within their lives. The person giving a prophecy is not responsible for what people do with the word; they are merely responsible for giving it.

13. Let love be your motivation.

This is possibly the most important principle of all. In the center of Paul's exhortation to the Corinthians concerning the gifts of the Spirit and the use of prophecy within the Church, he gives a poetic discourse on the agape love of God. He says that the most excellent path in the ministry of the gifts of the Spirit is the motivation of love. Our motive should not be to function within our gifting; it should always be to edify and build up the body of Christ. It is never about the delivery boy; it is all about what God desires to do within the life of the recipient. Love must be our motivation.

Word to the Wise

I have included only a partial list of things that should be practiced so that purity and integrity are established within the prophetic ministry. It is imperative to understand that prophecy is an important gift within the Church. It is God's voice flowing through a willing vessel, which has great ability to build and bless the body of Christ. However, when it becomes impure and is misused, it can bring destruction and reproach.

Many of the guidelines given in this chapter are derived from years of ministry experience. While there are no specific verses of Scripture that forbid anyone from putting a date or time on a prophetic word, it is wisdom to avoid it. Likewise, there is not a specific command that forbids election prophecies, but it is wise to steer clear of them because of the division they may bring. Since these are some of the areas that have caused controversy and confusion, we should at least be willing to take a step back and look introspectively. Paul said all things are lawful, but all things are not expedient.

As prophetic believers, we should make sure that we do everything we can to preserve the integrity of this important ministry. We must clean up the baby and then throw out the bathwater. There are far more good things that I have seen produced by the prophetic ministry than the errors recently demonstrated. We must all strive to maintain purity and accuracy within all the different manifestations of prophetic insight.

Let's return to doing things proper and right. We must maintain our focus on the purpose of the prophetic ministry within the Church: edify, exhort, and comfort. If we keep this at the forefront, along with proper prophetic principles by which to function, we will see prophetic integrity and purity established. As a result, believers will be built up and made strong as the voice of the Lord will breathe life into all those who hear it.

12
CONCLUSION

The different voices we have discussed within this book are the first and most important for a believer to be able to discern. These are foundational for the lives of believers. Failure to distinguish these voices properly can cause confusion. However, understanding of the manner in which these voices function and the language they speak brings clarity into our lives.

Everything begins with the knowledge that all that we hear is not correct. We will hear many things that are untrue and misleading. We have the responsibility to discern what is true from what is false. We must filter what is legitimate from what is illegitimate. This prevents the devil from taking advantage of us.

Human Makeup

The realization that we are a spirit, we have a soul, and we live in a body helps us in the processing of the different voices that we hear. Each part of our human makeup has a unique purpose. They each have a designated voice that must be properly distinguished so that correct and right decisions are made.

The spirit of man is the hub of spiritual existence. The soul of man is the hub of human existence. The body of man is the hub of physical existence. Proper understanding of the purpose of each part helps us in determining what voice to follow in different situations.

The voice of the flesh is the byproduct of the unrenewed mind and carnal appetites. Some of these appetites can be fostered by the physical body but is manifested because the mind has failed to be renewed. Everything that is done, good or bad, must pass through the mind of man. Therefore, it must be renewed and retrained. God's written and spoken Word along with the voice of the Spirit must become its master. We must fill ourselves with the Word of God and discipline our bodies so that we live a Spirit-ruled life. Our flesh must be crucified daily, and its voice silenced by the overwhelming power of the Word of God.

The Voice of the Holy Spirit

The Holy Spirit is alive and present within the lives of believers today. He makes His home inside of us. The Holy Spirit has a voice and speaks to us constantly in numerous ways. He speaks to confirm and affirm what Jesus said and is still saying. He comes to confront the things in our lives that need adjustment or removal. He is the voice of conviction that draws man to a place of repentance and change. His voice also convinces us of our redemption, and authority in Christ.

The prophetic voice of the Lord is needed in the Church today. It is not optional equipment for Christians, it is necessary, so believers become all that God has called them to be. The voice of prophecy is the testimony of Jesus within the Church. It will speak and say the things that align with the ministry of Jesus.

His voice will produce life and fruitfulness within all who hear and embrace it.

God uses prophets today to be His mouthpiece in the earth. They are one of the five-fold ministry gifts placed in the Church to equip believers to do the work of the ministry. The voice of the Lord released through prophets equip us to do and accomplish what God has declared.

Prophets speak and bones come together. Strength and foundation are produced within the Church as prophets yield to His anointing. This also generates the unity of the Spirit so that divine synergism can be released. Prophets give direction to the body of Christ as they speak the voice of the Lord. Their ministry is needed today and must be embraced for the Church to be everything God desires it to be.

Other Voices

There are many other voices that have not been discussed in this writing. Spiritual dreams and visions are legitimate voices whereby God gives direction to people. Angels and demons are spirit beings in the earth. Angels possess a legitimate voice and demons possess an illegitimate voice. One is God's messenger while the other is satan's servant. In my follow up book, *Voices of Deception*, I will discuss the different voices of the flesh and satan that seek to deceive Christians.

The voice of justification comes to give believers justification for sinful behavior. The voice of offense and bitterness destroys God-ordained relationships and provokes revenge. The voice of idols is the result of things within the heart of a Christian that have been given an exalted place above God and is given voice.

The voices of demons declare the lies of satan to enforce their master's bidding.

The voice of doubt will rob one of the promises of God. The voice of condemnation seeks to prevent the fulfilling of God's purpose and destiny within the lives of Christians. The voice of nonsense is the counterfeit that the enemy disguises to be the voice of the Lord. These are the voices that come to rob, steal, kill, and destroy. In my next writing, I will discuss all of these in detail so that we can guard ourselves from these heinous voices.

Take the teachings and enlightenment found in this book and let it help you correctly discern the voices that you hear. You were created to hear voices. It is not strange to hear them speak. Things will only become strange if we fail to properly distinguish the voices we hear. I pray that you will understand, recognize, and perceive the voices that you were made to hear and then follow the voice of the Good Shepherd. His voice will lead you in the path of life.

ABOUT THE AUTHOR

 **DR. ROBERT GAY** is Senior Pastor and Apostolic founder of High Praise Worship Center in Panama City, Florida. His ministry has a three-fold vision statement: Equipping Believers, Building Families, and Furthering the kingdom of God. Robert provides apostolic oversight to multiple High Praise churches within the United States. He is recognized by many as a prophetic and apostolic voice bringing balance and order into the church today. For complete bio, go to www.highpraisepc.com.

Silencing The Enemy With Praise
Pastor Robert Gay

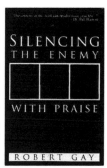

Praise and worship are more than words and music says author Pastor Robert Gay. Praise is a weapon of warfare. God will fight for you as you praise the greatness of His name.

"The contents of this book can revolutionize your life...It brings new understanding about the power of praise and worship."
-Dr. Bill Hamon

Planted
Pastor Robert Gay

Robert Gay confronts common "church issues" head on. He teaches with clarity and compassion that God is the Master Gardener who lovingly tends to every individual planted in His garden. You will find out how God wants to plant you so that you will flourish and grow and become everything He wants you to be.

"Every Pastor will appreciate this book...every saint of God should read this book..." - Dr. Bill Hamon

Best Of Robert Gay
Pastor Robert Gay

This compilation album represents some of Robert's most impactful songs that have touched the body of Christ throughout the world. This cd is packed full with 19 tracks that include powerful songs such as Mighty Man of War, Lord Sabaoth, On Bended Knee, Holy is Your Name, One Voice, No Other Name and much more!

Sonship
Pastor Joshua Gay

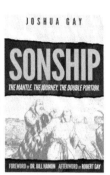

Discover the life of a true son through study of the Scripture and powerful testimonies. The author shines the light on many pitfalls that ensnare today's generation while revealing the true picture of faithful spiritual sons and daughters.

"This book needs to be read by every person who wants to be a true son or father according to God's order." - Dr. Bill Hamon

Faith Force Academy LIVE DVD
Volume 1: Meet The Faith Force

Join the Faith Force Heroes and Professors M & C in *Faith Force Academy LIVE!* as they teach you how to become strong superheroes of faith! This volume contains 4 exciting episodes that kids of all ages will be sure to enjoy. Each episode features exciting praise & worship, step by step teaching of scripture memory verses, incredible life-sized characters, & illustrated sermons.

Faith Force Academy LIVE DVD
Volume 2: Faith Is The Victory

Join the Faith Force Heroes and Professors M & C in *Faith Force Academy LIVE!* as they teach you how faith is our victory! This volume contains 4 exciting episodes that kids of all ages will be sure to enjoy. Each episode features exciting praise & worship, step by step teaching of scripture memory verses, incredible life-sized characters, & illustrated sermons.

Jesus In 3D
Pastor Robert Gay

Do you want to express the life of God in every aspect of your life? In your ministry? For us to walk in the totality of Jesus, we must first cherish the fullness of His ministry. Every dimension of the ministry of Jesus is critical for us to have ultimate effectiveness for the kingdom of God. Today, if you want to reflect the life of God, you must receive and activate all that He did, everything He said, and everything He demonstrated.

Revolutionaires
Pastor Joshua Gay

Revolutionaries declares to readers that God is raising up a transformation generation in the earth today. Discover the life of a spiritual revolutionary through the study of scripture and parallels from history.

"...if you read this book you are going to be enlightened, motivated and activated into being one of God's "Revolutionaries." - Dr. Bill Hamon

Building Strong
Pastor Robert Gay

There is a blueprint that the Father has rendered for the design of the Church. Jesus has been given the responsibility of building what was in the mind of the Father from creation. The Holy Spirit is the agent that empowers and gifts the spiritual subcontractors here on earth to build according to the plan that has been rendered from heaven.

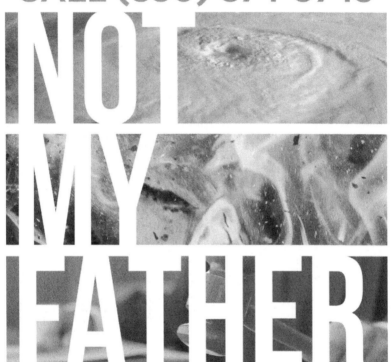

NOT MY FATHER

UNDERSTANDING GOD'S NATURE IN THE MIDST OF
STORMS, DISASTERS, AND JUDGMENT

ROBERT GAY

191